ANNA PAVORD'S GARDENING COMPANION

by the same author
The Flowering Year

ANNA PAVORD'S

GARDENING COMPANION

Chatto & Windus
LONDON

To Hilly Janes who set me on the road

Acknowledgements
All these pieces first appeared in the *Independent* newspaper and I am most grateful to the editor for allowing me to reprint them here. I am also delighted that Michael Daley allowed us to use some of his original illustrations. Timothy Leese kindly agreed to the reproduction of the plan on p227.
Rowena Skelton-Wallace has, once again, been an exemplary editor. I am enormously indebted to her, also to Penny David, Margaret Sadler and Pam Brown without whose expertise this book would never have been made.

Published in 1992 by
Chatto & Windus Ltd
20 Vauxhall Bridge Road
London SW1V 2SA

A CIP catalogue record for this book is available from the British Library

ISBN 0 7011 4953 1

Editor Penny David
Design Margaret Sadler
Chapter Opener Illustrations Michael Daley
Cover Illustration David Suff 'Poppy' hand-coloured etching 4 × 6in, Piccadilly Gallery, London, W1

Photoset by Rowland Phototypesetting Ltd
Bury St Edmunds, Suffolk
Printed and bound in Great Britain by
Butler & Tanner Ltd
Frome, Somerset

CONTENTS

J ANUARY

HOUSEPLANTS

One houseplant is all you need to purify the air in a hundred square feet of your home or office. This was the claim of David Foster, managing director of Greenscene, an interior landscaping company in Cheshire, on his return from Florida. He makes regular visits there to buy plants, but on this occasion came back weighed down with the results of a NASA (National Aeronautics and Space Administration) research project.

Their findings indicate that spider plants and mother-in-law's tongues are the best absorbents you can find for gobbling up unwanted formaldehyde. Ivy and dracaena are benzene addicts. Flowers such as gerbera and chrysanthemum specialize in filtering out trichloroethylene from the air.

NASA got involved in the research when they were looking for ways of purifying the atmosphere for scientists working in skylabs and space stations. When you are hurtling towards Mars in a tin can, however streamlined, opening windows is not an option.

Plants were an obvious choice because of their well-known ability to breathe in the carbon dioxide that we breathe out and turn it back into oxygen. The NASA researchers found that particular plants also dispose of other pollutants, absorbing them from the air through the tiny pores, or stomata, scattered over the surface of their leaves.

Even higher concentrations of toxic chemicals were assimilated by the roots of plants if the indoor air was filtered through a special compost with carbon granules mixed into it. David Foster's idea is to adapt the space-age research to try and solve a problem rather nearer home – the sick building syndrome.

'Sick' buildings are usually modern ones with closed ventilation systems. Sometimes the problem has an obvious source, as when the architect has thoughtfully placed the air-intake duct directly above a diesel lorry loading bay. Often it is a more complex cocktail of pollutants that gets into the air.

Formaldehyde leaks from foam insulation, plywood boards and carpets or upholstery made from synthetic fibres. The big drop in cigarette smoking has drastically cut down the amount of benzene floating round in the average office, but it is still escaping from the inks, oils and detergents that have become an essential part of everyday existence. Trichloroethylene is an essential ingredient of varnishes, lacquers and glues. All three may aggravate the symptoms shown by people who work in sick buildings: itchy eyes, sinus congestion, headaches, skin rashes.

Air, like water, used to be something you took for granted. You breathed it. It kept you alive. Occasionally your nose would signal that there was something weird going on that you couldn't see, but the problem with air is that, good or bad, it looks much the same.

In the energy-conscious era of the mid 1970s, air inside buildings often got forgotten in the stampede to conserve fuel. Foam insulation was pumped into cavity walls and roof spaces. Windows were double glazed. Opening a window became an anti-social act. Megalomanic architects designed office buildings that, just like space craft, locked their occupants into sealed chambers. Once in, you had to depend for sustenance on whatever blew out from the air ducts.

Gradually, it became clear that there was more to air conditioning than heating or cooling the stuff. In theory, it ought to be possible to provide air inside a building that is actually better than the curious soup that passes for air at street level in any city.

You should be able to filter out dust particles and the impurities that you cannot see. You should be able to dampen down the air, which in most offices feels as though it has come straight from the Sahara desert, and organize things so that fresh supplies of the stuff are regularly circulated round the building.

In practice it turned out to be more difficult than anyone supposed to regulate a decent air supply in a mostly sealed building, as Dr Tony Pickering at Wythenshawe Hospital, Manchester, discovered when he started his seminal research into the symptoms of 'sick' buildings. Specific causes have still to be pinned down. So have possible cures. The Pickering team have not yet looked at the question of plants and their effect on the office environment.

Plants certainly make you *feel* better about being trapped inside the relatively hostile environment of many offices. They give a semblance of normality, sometimes even of serenity. Professor Terry Mansfield of the University of Lancaster, the leading authority on gaseous pollutants and how they affect plants, believes that this may be the most important factor in making sure there are plenty of growing things in our homes and workplaces.

He had not seen the NASA research that so impressed Mr Foster. His own work has been chiefly in the area of plants and atmospheric contaminants such as sulphur dioxide. Plants, he pointed out, cannot avoid taking in whatever is offered to them in the surrounding atmosphere. Up to a certain limit they are remarkably tolerant of a wide range of strange additives. They had proved themselves to be very efficient sinks for all sorts of contaminants. They absorb them, detoxify them and then release them to be taken up in their normal metabolism.

The charcoal or active carbon in the soil was likely to have had as much effect in neutralizing the pollutants as the plants, said Professor Mansfield. He uses it in his own work when he is setting up experiments that require an atmosphere rid of all impurities. 'It works better when dry,' he added, 'so it would be even more effective if it was left out of the planting compost and stood in a pot on its own. It is a remarkable filter.'

Meanwhile David Foster blinds his Cheshire clients with science the Greenscene way. He has a £20,000 machine that can be wheeled into any suspect building to sample the air, an 'environmental audit' he calls it. Among other things this multi-gas analyser measures benzene, formaldehyde, carbon monoxide, carbon dioxide and water vapour, then spits out the number of parts of each in a measured quantity of air. 'It's very quick,' says Mr Foster; 'six gases in two minutes.'

From this analysis, he works out the right plants for the particular problems, and rents them to his customers, charging perhaps £12 a month for a container full. A bevy of plant valets makes regular calls to water and feed the plants, to polish leaves and generally keep them in trim.

The plants used in the original NASA research were chosen for their tolerance to low levels of light. These are also likely to be the plants that will flourish in the average modern office, where natural light is as rare as an opening window. All tropical foliage plants will grow better if their pots are kept standing on trays of damp pebbles. This extra humidity benefits us too.

The Nasa Team

Their formaldehyde fighters
Philodendron (Sweetheart plant)
Usually sold wrapped round a moss pole, but this climber can be used to trail out of a large container. It has pointed fleshy leaves and is untidy and formless, unless well trained. Pinch out the growing tips to make a bushy plant. Feed every two weeks in spring and summer, once a month in winter. Repot every spring in fresh compost.

Chlorophytum (Spider plant)
Possibly the commonest of all houseplants, usually seen in the variegated form with a cream stripe down the centre of each long thin leaf. Long stems spring from the base with new plantlets perched at the ends of the growths. They are very easy plants, tolerant of neglect, but respond to a feed given every two weeks. Repot every spring in fresh compost.

Rhapis (Bamboo palm)
Wide spreading fan-like leaves, made up of between five and nine segments. The plant is slow growing, taking several years to get to 4ft/1.2m. It needs space to display itself to the greatest advantage. Feed once a month while the plant is in active growth. Repot every two years using a soil-based compost.

Dracaena (Corn plant)
Slender spiky plants, a topknot of leaves springing like a fountain from a short woody stem. There are attractively variegated versions, with leaves variously striped in green, cream and pink. Feed every two weeks in spring and summer, more sparingly in winter. Repot in spring using a soil-based compost.

Sansevieria (Mother-in-law's tongue)
Broad, sword-shaped leaves, leathery in texture, with extremely sharp points. The growth is upright, dark green marbled and edged with gold. These are dramatic, bulky plants with strong architectural lines, suitable for ultra-modern interiors. They grow about 3ft/90cm high. Feed and water sparingly. Overwatering is the chief cause of death. Repot in spring, mixing perlite or coarse sand in the potting mixture to improve drainage.

Their benzene brigade
Hedera (English ivy)
An outdoor plant that puts up with indoor conditions remarkably well. It is useful for filling in at the front of planting groups as they are naturally graceful trailers, and they can, of course, be trained upwards over a support to give height to indoor plant displays. There are many different forms available, plain or variegated, large or small-leaved. Pinch out the grow-

ing tips to encourage bushy growth. Feed every two weeks in spring and summer, once a month in winter. Repot in spring, but only if the roots have filled all the space in the existing pot.

Spathiphyllum (Peace lily)
The flowers of these extraordinary plants are produced between May and August. They look like arums, but the texture is different, very waxy and unreal, the closest thing to plastic that the plant kingdom has yet discovered. There is a flat oval, the spathe, which can be white or pink or red, and then the spadix, which sticks out like a thumb from the centre. Feed every two weeks in spring and summer. Repot every two years using a peat-based compost. Humidity is essential if they are to grow properly.

Their trichloroethylene troops
Chrysanthemums
Often advertised cosily as 'Pot Mums' these are short-lived but colourful additions to more permanent displays of foliage plants. All the potted plants you buy have been treated with a growth-retarding hormone which ensures they stay at a manageable height. If you planted them in the garden, you would find in the succeeding season that the plants reached full height. A six-week display is the most you can expect from them.

GAMES OF TAG WITH KYLIE AND THE RECTOR

'No good can come of association with anything labelled Gwladys or Ysobel or Ethyl or Mabelle or Kathryn. But particularly Gwladys,' wrote P. G. Wodehouse. I have the same feeling about some plants. Is it possible to have an enduring relationship with a narcissus called 'Fairy Footsteps' or a rhododendron called 'Wee Willie'? I think not.

The naming of plants is a serious affair, ruled by the International Code of Nomenclature for Cultivated Plants. It is a subject of endless fascination to me. No dictionary yet exists to track down the history of 'Mrs Popple' the famous fuchsia or 'Maggie Mott' the mauve viola. Which Lady Elphinstone lent her name to a snowdrop, and why? What did Docteur Jamain do in 1865 to earn immortality by way of a rose?

Some names are easy to unravel. Breeders like to stamp their plants, as their children, with their own names. Among the sweet peas you will find plenty of Unwins: Sally, Charles, Alistair and Colin. The Ballard name is perpetuated in asters and hellebores and the Williams family of Caerhays lives on among camellias. Other names, such as the roses 'Ellen Willmott', 'Sissinghurst Castle' and 'Lawrence Johnston', commemorate famous gardeners and their gardens.

The present trend, to raid *TV Times* and *Radio*

Times for names, is rather less felicitous. There is quite enough of Terry Wogan around already without having him peeping winsomely from the garden in the guise of a sweet pea. 'Angela Rippon' makes an unlikely miniature rose and there is something unwholesome in the thought of crunching on a lettuce called 'Kylie'.

There is, of course, enormous commercial potential in choosing the right name for a plant. There is a vogue now for giving appropriate plants as presents. Robinias, gleditsias, golden ivies, hostas, the golden climbing hop, hollies and the mock orange *Philadelphus coronarius* 'Aureus' are favourites for golden weddings. Artemisias, ballota, elaeagnus, the silver-leaved pear and willow now cluster in a thousand gardens to commemorate a thousand marriages that against insuperable odds have staggered through to the 25-year mark.

I am also intrigued by the possibility of planting coded messages in the garden, perhaps the alstroemeria 'Margaret' surrounded by a planting of the sempervivum 'Twilight Blues'. One could incorporate some of the heavy moral messages that the Victorians liked to see in stained glass or illuminated manuscripts. Here the abies 'Prostrate Beauty' would be a natural, together with the rose 'Forgotten Dreams'.

Boot-lickers have ample scope for matching plants to people. The Army, the Navy and the Church are

Floral Tributes For All

Adam: Hedera, rose
Alexander: Clematis, rhododendron, rose
Alice: Bellis, dianthus, escallonia, passiflora
Alison: Chrysanthemum
Amy: Hebe
Andrew: Dianthus, fuchsia
Angela: Fuchsia
Annabel: Alstroemeria, clematis, fuchsia, helianthemum, hydrangea
Anne: Chrysanthemum, magnolia
Anthony: Pink
Barbara: Fuchsia, viola
Beatrix: Pelargonium, primula
Benedict: Pelargonium
Bridget: Chrysanthemum
Catherine: Primula
Celia: Pelargonium
Charles: Dianthus
Christabel: Hebe, viola
Christine: Dahlia, primula
Christopher: Dianthus
Clare: Dianthus, primula
Claudia: Chrysanthemum
Constance: Erica
Daphne: Chrysanthemum, pink, potentilla, rhododendron
David: Dianthus, fuchsia, rhododendron
Debbie: Camellia, chrysanthemum, fuchsia
Denis: Dianthus
Denise: Chrysanthemum
Diana: Aster, hedera, hibiscus

Diane: Hamamelis, narcissus, pelargonium, rhododendron
Edward: Dianthus
Eleanor: Pelargonium
Elizabeth: Aster, clematis, dianthus, fuchsia, gentian, magnolia, potentilla, rhododendron, viola
Ellen: Chrysanthemum, rose
Emily: Narcissus
Emma: Aster, viola
Erika: Chamaecyparis
Esther: Aster, saxifrage
Eva: Phlox, rose
Evelyn: Penstemon
Felicity: Aster, erigeron, viola
Fenella: Delphinium
Fiona: Dianthus, rose, viola
Frances: Erica
Gillian: Gladiolus
Hannah: Campanula
Helen: Chrysanthemum, dianthus, viola
Ian: Dianthus
Isobel: Campanula
James: Osteospermum
Janet: Dianthus, erica, hosta, primula, rhododendron, viola
Jenny: Aster, camellia, narcissus, primula, rhododendron
Jeremy: Pinus
Joanna: Primula
Jock: Rhododendron
Judy: Dianthus, magnolia
Julia: Aster, pelargonium, viola
Julian: Dianthus

Juliet: Chrysanthemum, rose
Karen: Aster, lewisia
Katherine: Malus
Katie: Camellia, dianthus, rose
Kitty: Camellia
Laura: Fuchsia, rose, viola
Louisa: Hosta, rhododendron
Louise: Chrysanthemum
Lorna: Delphinium
Lucinda: Camellia, fuchsia, viola
Lucy: Aster, aubrieta, viola
Lyn: Coprosma
Margaret: Alstroemeria, chrysanthemum, fuchsia, rose
Marjorie: Clematis, hebe
Marion: Primula
Mark: Primula
Mary: Aster, chrysanthemum, fuchsia, primula
Maureen: Clematis
Miranda: Campanula, dahlia, viola
Moira: Chrysanthemum
Monica: Rhododendron
Nancy: Aster
Naomi: Rhododendron
Nicola: Fuchsia, hosta
Oliver: Delphinium, iris
Olivia: Lily
Pamela: Aster, chrysanthemum, hippeastrum, viola
Pat: Cistus, primula
Patricia: Delphinium, dianthus, fuchsia, rhododendron, rose
Paul: Dianthus

Paula: Lewisia
Penelope: Aster, rhododendron, rose, saxifrage
Peter: Hedera
Rebecca: Aster, pelargonium
Richard: Buxus
Rita: Alstroemeria
Robert: Aster, bellis, dianthus
Rosalind: Deutzia, pernettya
Rosie: Pernettya
Sally: Hedera
Samantha: Delphinium, narcissus
Sarah: Alstroemeria, digitalis, narcissus, viola
Sheila: Chrysanthemum, pelargonium, primula
Shirley: Calluna
Sophie: Aster
Stella: Campanula, primula
Susan: Dianthus, halimiocistus, magnolia, rhododendron
Susannah: Dianthus
Suzanne: Hedera
Sylvia: Camellia, saxifrage
Tessa: Delphinium
Thomas: Dianthus
Timothy: Dianthus
Tony: Aster, narcissus
Trevor: Dianthus
Valerie: Fuchsia
Victoria: Alstroemeria, clematis, dianthus, erica, peony, viola
Wendy: Chrysanthemum, delphinium, hebe, pelargonium
Yvonne: Campanula, erica

all well represented in the nomenclature. Perhaps with these hierarchical professions, the most effective way to go about things is to pitch your gifts at the notch above the recipient. Give the bergenia 'Admiral' to a person who is only a Rear or a Vice. Send 'The Archbishop' aster to an ambitious bishop. The clergy feature heavily in plant lists and you will have no trouble in finding something to fit. 'Rambling Rector' (a rose) may fit all too well.

There is also the possibility of matching plants with pretensions. The argyranthemum 'Brontes' obviously needs a literary home. The rose 'Picasso' should go to the leading light of the local art society and the tulips 'Giuseppe Verdi' and 'Berlioz' be used to mollify the ruffled egos of competing tenors when auditions do not go their way.

Plants with more everyday Christian names, however, are ideal for godparents, distant aunts, stray cousins or megalomanic egotists to use when choosing plants as presents. The useful list on the previous pages will neatly solve the problem for the whole of the coming year: Mother's Day, birthdays, christenings, thank-you-for-having-me, Christmas. Men do not feature so heavily as women on the 'Floral Tributes' list, but you may be able to plug the gap with some broader category such as 'Banker' (dahlia) or 'Tubby' (campanula). Plenty of scope for coded messages here.

Resting on your Spotty Laurels

I don't suppose you could ever be passionate about spotty laurel (*Aucuba*). You don't swoop on it in the garden centre saying 'I've *always* wanted one of these!' You don't envisage a long period of mourning if it should die. Poor aucuba. There is nothing more dreary than being described as useful.

Its tragedy, of course, is that we take it too much for granted. It never looks as though it is going to keel over from ill health. It withstands frost, tempest and drought. It puts up with less than brilliant growing conditions. It is evergreen. It does not mind shade. The thing is a paragon, but still we do not love it.

Nor would I be without it. The bulk of it in winter, when so many things have shrivelled back to skeletons, is comforting. The colour, bright green flecked and streaked with gold, is warm in fog and frost. It is generally as wide as it is high, and will shield you permanently from views you would rather not see. It rarely gets above 10ft/3m. The branches are lax and arch outwards when they get heavy with leaves.

It needs no regular pruning. Because it has such large leaves, it looks better left unclipped. If you want to reduce its size, work on a branch at a time, tracing back the piece you want to get rid of to its junction with another branch and making the cut there.

Cutting back some of the growth on a regular basis stimulates a supply of fresh growth and this will have bigger and shinier leaves than those on old branches. April is the best time to do this, but aucuba is a forgiving plant and will excuse some snipping at any time of the year.

I attacked some of mine this autumn where it was lurching into the airspace of a nearby mahonia and forcing it to make an inelegant U-turn. Just in the one area where I was cutting, I came upon three birds' nests balanced on the aucuba's stems. The birds love its dark, dry undergrowth. They must like the red berries too, as none is now left on the bushes.

There are plain green aucubas and the female of one of them, A. *longifolia*, has some of the best berries of the tribe. If berries are important, you need male and female plants, though not necessarily next door to each other.

If you want a variegated aucuba, choose one that looks as though it is proud of its spots. 'Crotonifolia' is boldly blotched, generally male, though some plants have been known to bear berries. 'Picturata' has its variegation more under control, with a central golden blotch on each bright green leaf. It is male.

Aucubas make handsome tub plants, especially in town gardens, where you need as much foliage as possible to soften the overwhelming landscape of tar-mac, concrete and metal. So does the neat shrub osmanthus, especially in its form *Osmanthus hetero-phyllus* 'Variegatus'.

I picked this up at the excellent plant centre at the Royal Horticultural Society's garden at Wisley, Surrey, the sort of impulse purchase that gardening writers warn you against. I liked its leaf, dark, ever-green, jagged, rather like a holly leaf, but not as prickly and edged in an absent-minded way with cream. Since I had no particular place for it in mind, I stuck it in a large pot when I came home and there it has remained. It gives bulk to the mainly evanescent display in the pots by the back door. It fills its corner boldly. This spring it acquired a skirt of daisy-flowered erigerons round its base. Both are in permanent shade, north-facing.

After eighteen months in its pot, with never a hiccup, I feel I can recommend it wholeheartedly. It is growing, but slowly, and it is making a rounded bush, as wide as it is high. It is more compact than other forms, but shyer to flower. I do not mind that. I bought it for its leaves. It does not need regular pruning, but if it began to look lopsided then I would

snip at it and take out a branch or two in April.

Evergreen trees are as essential as shrubs, but where, as is often the case, there is room for only one, the choice is more difficult. Yew, holly, box, bay and ilex are my own favourites, though they will not be with those who want quick results. Mine came with the house. If you are as lucky, leave them time to grow on you before you whip out the chain saw.

Yew, although usually confined within the strait-jacket of a hedge, makes a magnificent specimen tree, but it must only be put in a place big enough to contain it for the next thousand years. It is too wide-spreading for small gardens, except in the form dis-covered in Ireland, the upright *Taxus baccata* 'Fastigiata'. I can see that looking very good at the end of a path in a small garden.

Box is even more rarely planted as a tree than yew. It rarely gets above 10–12ft/3–3.5m and is rather narrow. The side branches do not stray far from the main trunk. It is most interesting when allowed to grow as a multi-stemmed tree, with the foliage gath-ered – clipped, even – in clouds on the branches. The bark is pale, creamy and furrowed. The wood inside is very tight-grained, which is why box is so highly favoured by wood engravers.

It will grow best in places where it has plenty of air and light, though it will put up with worse. It also needs feeding. Mulch it liberally every autumn with whatever bulky manure you can lay your hands on. And wait. It will take sixty years or more to reach its full potential.

Oaks are not renowned for speediness either, but you can die happy once you have planted an oak. Like any other proper tree, it is a gift to the future. The ilex or holm oak (*Quercus ilex*) has evergreen leaves, matt rather than shiny, thin and pointed like an olive leaf. The undersides are pale green-grey. Its resemblance to our own native oak seems rather obscure.

Given the space, it makes a large tree with a rounded head, but it can also insinuate itself among other neighbours and snake up to the light, making a much narrower shape. It is hardy, but does not thrive in the coldest areas of the country. You find it most often in coastal areas, for it is highly resistant to salt-laden winds.

Oaks can be tricky to establish and sometimes sulk for the first couple of years after planting. Do not expect them to put up with poor dry soils. Mulch and water them well. If you want to grow oaks from acorns, plant them as soon as you can after gathering them. Although not a native, the holm oak has been cultivated in this country since the sixteenth century. There is a superb double avenue of them, with clipped heads, in the garden at Hatfield House in Hertfordshire.

NOVICE GARDENERS: PART ONE
FORETHOUGHTFUL

Plants should come a long way down the list of priorities for the novice gardener. There are many things to think about before even the first tentative daffodil bulb is sunk into the ground. January is a good time to do this kind of thinking: you can't do much else. The first and most important question to mull over as you gaze at your patch is: what is this garden for?

If you start writing down some of the responses to that question, you will find you have along the way acquired a ragbag of elements that will have an important bearing on the design. If there are small children in the equation, there will need to be a flat, soft area where they can fall off swings and climbing frames. If you like hanging out washing rather than drying it in the bowels of an expensive machine, you will need a line and a dry path to get to and from it.

Some novice gardeners may not want to do much actual gardening at all, but, conversely, do not want to look out every day over a scene of threadbare grass and rotting fence. Their ideal garden will look good and demand little attention. If you are a dedicated sun-worshipper, you need to mark out the part of the garden where the sun lingers longest. It may not be the part nearest the house, though this is where sitting out areas tend to be made.

You may, even as a novice, care so passionately about plants that all you want is the maximum space to grow them in. Raised beds built down an unpromising alley could provide extra gardening space.

Privacy is an important consideration. A first-time garden is usually small and certainly the typical one I am imagining is no more than 40 × 20ft/12 × 6m and surrounded on all sides by other houses and their gardens. Privacy is a ticklish business where close neighbours are concerned. To throw up an impenetrable Berlin Wall between you and them could be tactless. Trellis is a useful compromise and you can always pretend it was forced on you by the speed of growth of your climbing rose.

Aesthetes among the novices will by now be thoroughly irritable and complaining that gardens should have as much to do with the soul as with the necessity of a washing line or a barbecue pit. So they should, and when the list of necessities is securely written down, you can ask the second question: How do I want this garden to feel?

This question produces as varied a response as the first. Some urban gardeners, as short of space inside as they are out, want their gardens to be extensions of their homes, with a great deal of hard paving, good furniture and lighting. The garden for them should feel like an extra sitting room, gnat-ridden perhaps, damp occasionally, but an important overflow of

living space. Closet countrysiders may want to pretend their patch is actually a corner of some Sussex
meadow and picture it swagged with honeysuckle and
waving with ox-eye daisies and scabious – difficult to
bring off with suburban trains hurtling by.

A leafy retreat is an excellent goal for a small town
garden, but it is best made acknowledging the urban
setting, using un-wild plants such as bamboo,
acanthus, fig, vine, alchemilla, euphorbia, wisteria.

While you are working through this process, take
note of the features in the garden that you would like
to keep. On a new estate, there may be nothing. In
an old garden, there may be a fruit tree, or a good
bulwark of evergreen laurel or box that, tidied up,
could add a dash of venerability to the new garden
that will emerge around it. If you do not know what
a tree or shrub is, give it a year's grace to demonstrate
its worth before you take up the axe.

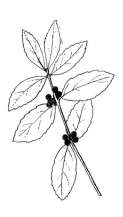

The mood of the garden will dictate its eventual
style. It may be clipped classical, random cottage,
modern high-tech, or some intensely personal vision
which exists in your head and wants to get out. Do
not let anybody, particularly gardening writers, tread
on your dreams.

All this thinking and doodling will not have
changed the view outside the window, but it is a vital
part of the gardening process. Before you can make,
you have to know what it is you are making.

JOBS FOR THE MONTH

General

🌣 Prepare for the new season by washing pots and seed trays ready for re-use.

🌣 Continue to dig over soil outside when the weather allows.

🌣 Cut back overgrown deciduous hedges. Aim for a shape that is wider at the bottom than the top. This allows light to reach the lower branches more easily. Pull out any perennial weeds from the bottom of the hedge.

🌣 Check staked trees and adjust the ties if necessary. The aim is to support the trunk, not throttle it.

🌣 Prune overgrown laurel, cutting back hard with saw or secateurs.

🌣 Overhaul mowers by cleaning the air filter and the spark plug. Mechanics *manqués* will also drain and replace the engine oil. Or you can pass the buck and take the mower to the service engineers.

🌣 Brush off snow from shrubs and trees before it settles and freezes. The weight may cause branches to crack.

🌣 Prune and train ornamental vines such as *Vitis coignetiae* and 'Brant' which are growing on walls or pergolas.

🌣 Protect fish and garden pools by ensuring there is always an ice-free area on the surface of the water.

Flowers

🌣 If you are planning to grow dahlias, dig plenty of muck into the patch where you want to plant them. Dahlias are hungry feeders and will thrive only in rich ground.

🌣 Remove any dying leaves from pelargonium cuttings.

🌣 Order flower seed. Catalogues make heady reading in the drab, damp days of January. Ageratums are useful half-hardy annuals, usually not more than 12in/30cm high, with neat powder-puff clumps of flowers in shades of lavender blue and pink. They flower well even in a murky summer and the blue varieties make an excellent edging mixed with creamy helianthemums. Late blooms also look good under the purple berries of *Callicarpa bodinieri*. Sow seed in March, set out plants in late May to have flowers by July.

❧ Biennials take longer to come into flower. They spend the first year building themselves up, then flower from spring in the year after they were sown. Try a foxglove such as Suttons' 'Apricot', which has tall spires of a glorious soft apricot colour. They prefer cool, damp growing conditions. They look good mixed with honesty, another biennial, especially the variegated *Lunaria annua variegata*.

Vegetables
❧ Sow greenhouse tomatoes towards the end of the month.
❧ Order seed ready for planting later in the year. *The Vegetable Finder*, published by the Henry Doubleday Research Association, will help you to track down unusual varieties. For guidance on the best varieties to grow, get hold of the Wisley handbook *Vegetable Varieties for the Gardener*.

Fruit
❧ Check apples in store regularly and remove any that are rotting.
❧ Mulch gooseberry bushes with plenty of well-rotted manure or compost.
❧ Continue to prune established fruit trees where necessary.
❧ Plant rhubarb. Plants should be positioned at least 3ft/90cm apart. Set the crowns about 1in/2.5cm below the surface of the soil and then spread strawy manure round each crown.

F EBRUARY

Cultivating Personalities

Psychoanalysts may yet discover an important diagnostic tool in the matter of gardens and children. The different gardens that our three children made are turning out to be curiously accurate indicators of their personalities.

The youngest child gardened only for profit, growing vast quantities of mustard and cress, radishes, lettuces and tomatoes. These, keenly priced, were set out on a table by the back gate together with posies of flowers. A pipe led down through the palings into a bucket our side of the gate. A heavily embellished notice pinned to the table instructed passers-by to 'Put Munny in Pipe'. To my astonishment and her delight, several did. Any produce remaining at the end of the day was usually pressed upon me, at only a small discount.

The middle child made a weed garden, choosing a favoured piece of land in a south-facing border, so as to give the weeds the best possible chance in life. To this sunny, well dug, well fed plot, she brought all the different weeds she could find in the garden, carefully transplanting them and nourishing them with special elixirs of her own making. Making the mixtures, pounding up dandelion petals with rain water from the butt, garnished with a sprinkling of parsley or sage, was an important part of the process.

26

As gardening lost its charm, she transferred her attentions to other underdogs, joining Amnesty International, becoming – temporarily – a vegetarian and introducing words like radical, ethnocentric and alternative lifestyle into family conversation.

The eldest child, as is so often the fate of eldest children, did everything that she should. She tended her plot conscientiously, put a bird bath in the middle of it, edged it with shells, weeded fanatically, dead-headed, even got her strawberries to fruit when my own patch was a complete washout. It seemed at the time to give her pleasure and looking back on it now, she thinks it did too. Order from chaos seemed to be her driving force. At a time when most of the rest of the garden was a wilderness, her small square was a sheet anchor.

Whatever the reasons that draw children into gardening, by the age of thirteen, only a minute hard core will still be interested and then usually in one specific kind of plant – cacti perhaps, or carnivorous plants.

Even though the span may be short, learning to respect plants and their needs is important. It leads to a wider respect for the way that the world is put together. This of course is not the kind of heavy preaching that you ought to go in for while your offspring is tending his sunflowers. The messages that come through gardening are subliminal.

27

As with all things to do with children, gardening
will not grab them just because you, the parent, think
that it is a good thing that it should. If you are
interested yourself, it is most likely that your children, while they are small and much with you, will
also want to be involved. For a while it seems they
only want to stick their trowels in precisely the same
spot as your own is busy. This is the most frustrating
stage for both parties. All you can do is hang on for
the good times and, in a low, calm voice, hone
further your explanation of *why* they should not pull
up young plants to see how the roots are growing.

The more interesting stage comes later, round
about four or five years old, when children want their
own plots. Size and situation are very important.
Although you may grit your teeth when handing it
over, a child's plot needs to be on good soil and in
an open situation. If it is stuck in a corner under a
privet hedge, discouragement is inevitable. If it is too
small, there will not be enough scope for experiment.
If too big, it will become a chore rather than a pleasure. A space with room for expansion is ideal.

Edging, marking the boundaries, seems to be very
important to children, so you need plenty of bits and
pieces to hand for this task: pebbles, slivers of wood,
scallop shells if you live in that sort of *nouvelle cuisine*
home, broken brick if you don't.

I feel it is best to distinguish clearly between matters of fact and matters of taste when you are called on for advice. In the case of sowing seed, certain principles must be grasped and followed. In the matter of planting orange French marigolds among purple pansies, children must follow their own noses and do what delights them.

Tools should be real tools, even though a trowel may look like a miner's shovel in the hands of a four-year-old. It is important for them to feel that you are treating their garden seriously. Scaled-down, doll's-house tools that buckle at their first encounter with a stone do not give this impression.

As for plants, pansies are excellent starting points, universally appealing, it seems, and of strong constitution. This matters. A child's garden is no place for a sickly, demanding plant. Choose those that can cheerfully surmount the perils of being over or underwatered and handled with the dexterity of a prize fighter with his gloves on.

Fast-growing plants are a boon, as the long-drawn-out nature of most of the processes of gardening is what children find difficult to grasp. Sunflowers are excellent if you have room. Sweet peas are also satisfying, as they can be started in pots inside and planted out against a wigwam of canes when they have outgrown the kitchen windowsill. Any plant that needs more than merely planting is useful. Sunflowers are not much help here, but pansies need picking over frequently. So do sweet peas.

The mixtures of annual flowers specially packaged for children have not been a success as far as our mob is concerned. The pictures on the packets encourage expectations rather rosier than reality. Broadcasting seed straight on to the ground is not a sure enough method of success for children. Buy plants to give the bulk of the flowers and for the rest, stick to big seeds, such as nasturtium, that can be handled easily or grown singly in pots inside and transplanted later.

Food goes down well in children's gardens. Growing it, that is. Radishes are rapid, but unpalatable to many. Tomatoes are slow, but rate high in the amount of titivating that can go on around them, nipping off side shoots, adding more ties to the stake. As they go up rather than out, they are especially valuable where space is limited.

For small children, mustard and cress is unbeatable. Egomania can be gratified temporarily by the sight of their initials growing in mustard and cress. The crunch comes when you suggest cutting some for a salad. Which bit of themselves can they amputate?

A different kind of megalomaniac child enjoys growing monster marrows, but you need space. One plant will take up about 2 × 2ft/60 × 60cm. There is a pleasantly mythical quality about marrows and pumpkins and the metamorphoses that might occur in the night. You can carve your initials on a marrow too, and watch them get bigger and bigger as the vegetable grows.

There is another side to gardening with children of course. This has to do with tulips falling in a flail of airgun pellets, of footballs through greenhouse windows and a mudslide where you once remembered a lawn. The most cataclysmic gardening event of my own childhood was the experiment my brother carried out with home-made gunpowder and a cocoa tin. It blew a crater worthy of the Western Front in the lawn, but he passed his chemistry exam with flying colours.

❧❀⊛❀☙

BORDER RAID

In a sudden fit of irritation recently, I recklessly tore out all the plants from a front border. It had never been right but, in the rather despairing way that one puts new cushions on a foul sofa, I had been trying to jolly it along with occasional offerings of new plants.

The problem started many years ago, when we first moved to the house in 1974. It had been uninhabited for years. Ivy grew up the walls – inside. The outside was an impenetrable thicket of bramble, elder and other dross. I had become hooked on gardening at our first house and, when we moved, brought some of the plants that I had become fond of there: iris, madonna lilies, peony, alstroemeria, delphiniums.

Faced with an acre and a half of jungle and the usual complement of small children that seem to go with house-moving, I dug a panic border along the south-facing front of the house. The border is broken into halves by the porch and front door. Each half is roughly 20ft/6m long. The width was dictated by the fact that I struck rubble about 4ft/1.2m out from the house wall, the foundations of the driveway that had once gone right round the house.

Into this border I dumped the booty I had brought with me. It never recovered from this hasty start. Paradoxically, the general effect was made worse by the fact that this border was one of the most favoured spots in the garden: warm and sheltered, with excel-lent free-draining soil. All the tender plants that I experimented with over the succeeding years – felicias, salvias, osteospermums, argyranthemums – had to go in this border because nowhere else suited them so well.

Individually the plants were fine. Altogether the effect was a polka-dot mess. And, as the rest of the garden developed, I began to feel that some areas could do with more discipline. All this led up to the grand wrecking of the right-hand border.

My idea was for a type of ribbon border, popular in Victorian times, deeply unfashionable now. I wanted to try plants of the same type planted in parallel rows along the front border, in a way that might suit the symmetrical sash-windowed front. All through the winter I have been rolling various combinations around in my mind.

The background is blue and white: a *Wisteria venusta* 'Alba' planted in 1975 between the front door and the window and a clematis, 'Mrs Cholmondeley', between the window and the end of the house. The clematis had originally scrambled through a massive evergreen ceanothus, 'Trewithen Blue', planted in 1977, but we lost that in a freak November gale. I am planting another in its place.

The presence or absence of yellow is as far as I usually get in colour planning. Since in the rest of the garden it is present more than not, I thought this new border could do without it. I also, for nostalgic reasons, decided to use the tall *Iris ochroleuca* that had been in the border since the original dump. These are 4ft/1.2m high, with good tall spear-like leaves growing straight up from the rhizome, rather than in a fan like bearded iris. The flowers are white (with a bold yellow blotch) and beardless, opening in succession from a single stem. These are now lined out along the back of the border against the house wall. I was also thinking of them vaguely as support, for in front I have planted a line of gypsophila, which may be a mistake. It is G. *paniculata* 'Bristol Fairy' with double white flowers. It grows brilliantly in a Lincolnshire garden that we look after, billowing great clouds of flowers into the border for a long period between June and August.

The Lincolnshire soil is very sandy and I am not convinced that the gypsophila will do as well in Dorset. It is worth a try. It was a favourite plant of Gertrude Jekyll's, but she had sandy soil too. It may also flop in the wrong direction.

In front of the gypsophila, *Penstemon* 'Sour Grapes'. I was looking for something that would take the border through August. Height was a consideration in the choice of varieties. I did not want anything too tall, nor did I want more of 'Garnet' or 'Ruby', which have already afforested other parts of the garden.

In a thick jagged band between iris, gypsophila and penstemon, I have planted the parrot tulip 'Estelle Rijnveld', an old favourite and a mad one, with jagged petals of rich raspberry splashed and streaked with white. The tulips unfortunately do not last many seasons, but fresh plantings, choosing different varieties, will give the border a fillip. These plants, taking into account the wall cover, give me a reasonably good season from late April to September. I am not looking here for winter interest. There is a winter border just round the corner with mahonia, cyclamen, hellebores and ivy. Next season I may plant the front border thickly with three different kinds of

Crocus chrysanthus. A hundred each of 'Snow Bunting', 'Blue Bird' and 'Blue Pearl' would do, the white in the middle, merging into blue either side. That would take care of March.

The thing that really worries me about the ribbon border so far is the lack of bulk, the lack of something with excellent foliage. The iris is good, but not excellent, while the gypsophila and penstemon are both messy. Most of the bulky foliage plants I like best would not enjoy this hot spot, but something is needed to fit in between the penstemon and the front row of plants, which will probably be violas.

The uncertainty about the in-between strand has temporarily halted planting. I will probably finish off the front edge with *Viola* 'Boughton Blue' this spring. I have found it impressively exuberant with a long season of sky-blue flowers.

The type of plant I have in mind cuts out a whole swathe of greys, such as artemisias, that would enjoy this billet, but they are too fussy. I want something that looks more edible, something with a bulkier leaf. Hostas came briefly to mind, then passed on. Eryngiums stayed longer. The prickly flower heads would be an advantage late in the season.

Herbaceous geraniums are bulky and the greyish-leaved *Geranium renardii* is a possibility. It is not too vigorous, a problem which cuts out many others of this type of geranium. Nor is it too tall. It has rather grubby-looking lavender flowers. I could also use one of the small magenta-flowered geraniums such as 'Ballerina'. One has the better leaf, the other the better flower.

Another idea, stolen from Clough Williams-Ellis's garden at Plas Brondanw in North Wales, would be to use a cabbagy succulent such as echeveria, bedded out along the border. These have the thick juicy texture of sedums or ice plants, but are perfectly symmetrical – neat fat rosettes of glaucous blue-green, up to 10in/25cm across, sitting on the ground. The disadvantage of echeverias is that they are tender and would need to be dug up and stored somewhere frost-free over winter. On the other hand, think of the advantages – the strangeness, the sense of surprise. Hang geraniums. I think this may be an echeveria summer.

❧❦❧

BASIL

The last basil plant of summer has finally turned up its toes on the kitchen windowsill. Its companions, a stalwart half-dozen, have been giving up at intervals since mid-December. I shall be bereft without them.

Even the most hastily constructed salad or dish of pasta is transformed by a whiff of basil. I am irritated that I never got round to the olive oil trick. Pack basil leaves into a jar, pour oil on top and leave it to steep for two weeks, before draining. You then have richly scented olive oil to use in salad dressings.

The plants were grown from seed sown in April. I used ordinary potting compost, although some people find that compost mixed with perlite gives better results. Cover the pot with glass or clingfilm until the seedlings emerge.

Mine were pricked out into square 3in/7.5cm pots and stayed there, spending their whole lives on the kitchen windowsill, in the company of hirsute begonia, some seedlings of giant fennel and the usual collection of odd buttons, screws, corks and safety pins that experience has taught should never be thrown away. From time to time the whole lot spent a night soaking in the sink, the water beefed up with a touch of Baby Bio. They try to flower but you must not let them. Pinch out the flower heads to keep a good supply of leaves coming on.

I used ordinary sweet basil (*Ocimum basilicum*) from Suffolk Herbs. They call it Genovese basil, and it is one of fourteen different kinds listed in their cata-logue. Half a packet sown will provide plenty of plants to give away. In the north, the windowsill treatment, or a greenhouse or polytunnel, will be the best way to grow them. In the south, you can risk sowing outside.

The lazy way is to delay sowing until mid-June, so

that by the time the plants come up, their surroundings bear a passing resemblance to the balmy conditions they remember from home. However, you will not get plants early enough to make best use of them, even if you sow (as you must) in a warm, sheltered spot.

If you sow earlier, you need to give the plants protection. John and Caryl Hubbard, who had the best basil bed I had ever seen in their Chilcombe garden when I visited, sow seed at the beginning of May but keep the ground covered with cloches until the nights are warm. The plants must be gradually acclimatized. If you get it wrong, the leaves turn a dramatic black overnight. There is a lot of fiddling with this method. The cloches have to be shifted whenever you water and also if the sun gets hot during the day. Caryl is thinking instead of using a floating mulch (Agryl) to protect the plants.

She grew a cinnamon basil from Mexico, a lemon basil from Indonesia and another one with purple leaves and pink flowers called 'Dark Opal'. She has also tried the ruffled varieties, both the green and the purple with leaves that are crinkled and fringed. The flavour is much the same as the ordinary basil. All are available from Suffolk Herbs, or from the Henry Doubleday Research Association (HDRA) Heritage Seed list. All are annuals.

If you sow direct into the soil, you need to thin

the seedlings as they develop so that they are eventually about 12in/30cm apart. Left to themselves, most types leap straight up in a single stem. If you pinch out the growing top, you can persuade them to make bushier, leafier plants. Greek basil, which is the only other type I have ever grown, is by nature more bushy. Whereas the Genovese type makes a plant at least 18in/45cm tall, the Greek is half that height, with tiny leaves. It is excellent in pots, as it looks like a small topiary tree, ball-shaped and prolific. You can freeze whole heads of this Greek basil. The flavour hangs on better with freezing than with drying. The leaves go crisp and you can crumble them into soups and stews.

This year I am going basil mad and am growing seven different sorts. This is the sort of thing that happens when you get a really interesting seed list, such as the ones produced by Suffolk Herbs and the HDRA. Chiltern's is another catalogue that can be read like a book. Their vegetables, although sound, are more of an afterthought to the flowers, but they have a strong section on oriental vegetables.

Mizuna is the only oriental I grew this year. It has elegant bright green leaves, deeply cut and fringed. It would be very pretty growing in a large pot with lobelia. It is a salady sort of thing. You pick a few leaves when you need them. It has stood up to the cold well and is still growing lustily outside without any protection. As with lettuce, its taste is difficult to describe, but it is useful to throw into a hotch-potch of leaves at this time of the year.

Radicchio, a type of chicory, has also been useful through the winter, producing a succulent succession of tiny new leaves, the colour of port wine. Suttons list it simply as radicchio, but it is probably 'Rossa di Verona' as its leaves curl over to make soft ball shapes.

I sowed seed in a drill outside on 13 May. During the summer I rather forgot it as there was so much else to eat. But now I am very grateful for it. It is too bitter to use on its own, but adds a sharp edge and good colour to mixed salads. It works as a short-lived perennial. At the end of summer it throws up tall flowering spikes, covered with flowers of powderpuff blue. Then you cut the whole plant back and in the new year it begins to sprout the most succulent small leaves. Like the mizuna, it has had no protection. Thin the plants in the row to 9in/23cm apart.

This vegetable is the speciality of the north-east region of Italy, where each town has its own variety. Suffolk Herbs has seven different kinds, including several decorative variegated types. 'Variegata di Castelfranco' is green and red in summer, red and white in cold weather. 'Variegata di Chioggia' has leaves that are green in summer, turning mottled red and white in winter. Like the one I have been growing, it does not need forcing. 'Castelfranco' does, for best results.

Watercress is another winter delight. We made regular forays as children to gather it from a stream at the farm in Wales where my mother was born. Nobody fussed about liver fluke then. Only one rule was bashed into us: we must gather watercress only from places where the water was moving. The other difficulty was brooklime (*Veronica beccabunga*) which resembles watercress, grows in the same places and which we thought poisonous.

Wild watercress has smaller leaves than the culti-vated kinds and is bronze rather than dark green. Fortunately, I have located another excellent source of the wild stuff and picked an icy bunch last week. The rosettes splay out flatly, the most succulent bits sticking out above the water. My fingers practically dropped off with cold, but it does not take long to gather enough for a salad or a soup. One of my favour-ite winter soups is potato and watercress, enriched with some dollops of Jersey cream from the farm down the road.

Watercress is listed in several seed catalogues, with the note that it does not *have* to have water to grow. It needs a rich, moist, cool soil, though I have never seen it growing this way. It is a phenomenally healthy vegetable. We were fed it in copious quantities because of its iron – one of my mother's little obsessions – but watercress is also bursting with vitamins: mostly C, but also A and B, with trace elements of copper and calcium.

Most of the instructions in old books are for growing it in water, but one suggests planting slips (small rooted pieces) in September in a moist, shady bed. 'Dig the earth fine,' it says; 'draw a slight trench with a hoe, fill this with water until it becomes a mud, cover it about an inch deep with sand and then stick in the slips about six inches apart, watering them until established.'

The book suggests that the flavour is not so mild as that of water-grown cress. You can also grow plants from seed, scattering it in a narrow damp trench, as above, and then thinning the plants once they have germinated. From an April sowing you could expect to be picking watercress in autumn. Real watercress, of course, is an entirely different vegetable to American land cress. Watercress is a member of the nasturtium family, which seems odd until you remember the taste of young nasturtium leaves in summer sandwiches. They have a similar spicy tang.

NOVICE GARDENERS: PART TWO
GROUND LEVEL DESIGN

Faced with a plot of ground to turn into a garden, a new gardener's instinct is to tackle the edges first, to work round the boundary. Perhaps this is a remnant of some atavistic urge to mark territory. Dogs lift legs. We plant clematis. Whatever the reason, it usually leads to a particular sort of garden layout: borders, usually too narrow to build up any depth in plant groups, all the way round the edge of the plot, path making another circuit round the inside edge of the borders, or, if money and energy run out, leading up just one side of the plot, parallel with the boundary. There will be a bit of terracing next to the house. Whatever ground is left becomes lawn. The centre of a design such as this becomes a centre by default, not so much a designed shape as a random happening.

If you think from the centre of the space out towards the boundaries, quite different patterns may begin to emerge. You may start with the thought of a rectangular paved area in the middle of the plot, with wide flower borders on either side reaching to the boundaries. You may see a path up through the centre of the garden, the length divided by upright screens of trellis either side of the path so that the width of the garden spreads and narrows as you pass down the path between the trellis screens and into the spaces contained beyond them. There could be rectangles of grass either side of the central path, with plants contained in raised beds round the three-sided shapes made by the trellis screens and the boundary wall. (Do not think of raised beds against a fence. The weight of the earth will gradually force it to collapse – into your neighbour's garden.)

These are simple ways of manipulating shapes on the ground, using the same basic ingredients of paths, flower beds and grass that regularly crop up in outside gardens. By thinking of the centre first, you may end up with an arrangement that gives you far more opportunities for imaginative planting and consequently more pleasure.

Novice gardeners are usually told they must draw out a plan on paper before they start flailing around with spades and wheelbarrows. Because this is the way professional garden designers work, it has been assumed that it is also the best way forward for amateurs. It ain't necessarily so.

The first path in our present garden was made by my brother, a vet and a superb gardener. On one of his rare weekends off, he came down to our patch, an acre and a half of garden wilderness untouched for twenty years, specifically to undertake this project. I was hugely excited. Marooned inside by small children who hung on to my legs for most of their waking hours, I watched from the kitchen window.

My brother stood on the bank and gazed out at the view. Several hours later he was sitting on a log gazing at the view. At the end of the first day, not a sod had been turned. On Sunday, I decided that the path was a lost cause. My brother spent most of the morning staring up into a beech tree, rubbing his nose. 'He needs the rest,' I said, to no one in particular. We had lunch. I spent the afternoon at the beach, and returned to find my brother gone. But there, as you will have been expecting, was the path.

It was wider than I would ever have planned on paper, although on the ground it looked absolutely in scale. It also took a line that I would never have thought of drawing, but which brought it around a tricky contour and gave a nice glimpse of a beech tree lined up with an ilex along the way. I cannot pretend that anything that has happened in the garden since has been worked out on paper first.

Paper designs tend to get over-complicated. Interlocking circles ooze out over the page. A bare space is a threat to your creativity. The obvious is avoided at all costs. 'Features', as designers call them, start bobbing up all over the place. To achieve its full effect, a feature should be used as sparingly as a threat.

Another difficulty with paper is that it cannot contain the information you need to make the right decisions and which you get as you prowl over your

patch. You take in the slight rises and falls in the ground and the consequences that these will have on your design. You are aware of things beyond your boundary that you would rather not see, and can work out more easily how this can be done.

Above all, working on the ground, it is easier to develop a sense of proportion and understand that a space where nothing is happening, a void, may be as important as anything else. A planned void is a very different thing to a void by default.

Professional designers would never get clients to pay for a couple of days walking about rubbing their noses. Time is the advantage amateurs have and when it has been well spent, mulling over possibilities and adaptations, sticks and string and hosepipe on the ground may prove better design tools than pencil and paper.

Having arranged the horizontal plane of your garden into a series of satisfying interlocking shapes, the next task will be to colour them in, like a Mondrian painting. To grass or not to grass is the first big question. My own feeling is that the smaller the garden, the less case there is for a lawn. Grass is restful. It provides a useful buffer and contrast between other more frenetic areas of plant activity, but it is demanding.

If you have small children, perhaps you feel you need a lawn for them, but grass quickly becomes threadbare under swings and climbing frames. An area thickly mulched with bark chippings might be a more practical alternative. You could compensate for the lack of green-ness by surrounding the patch with plenty of good foliage plants – ivy, fatsia, fig, choisya, all robust enough to survive some buffeting.

Fine gravel can be used as a surface finish instead of grass. Plants will seed themselves into it, bulbs will grow through it. This may be the effect you are after. If you like the idea of gravel, but want to retain it as a formal, clean, unplanted area, lay a plastic membrane on top of the earth and put the gravel on top of that. Different gravels give different colours and textures. Stick to one kind, but make sure it tones in with the colour and texture of the brick or stone around you.

Asphalt is perhaps the most unpleasant surface to look at in a garden. Concrete runs it a close second and has been in the past a favourite way of making the path round the lawn. Laid on an uneven surface, it cracks and splits and becomes as lethal as it is unsightly. If you have got one of those in your back garden, abandon all hopes of repairing it. Invite round a couple of aggrieved friends and get them to work out their spleen by smashing up the old concrete, which you can then cart off to the tip.

Bark is good for paths as well as children's play areas, though not for both, or your garden will begin to look like a demonstration plot for the Forestry Commission's waste products. Contrast in texture is what you are after on the different flat surfaces of the garden. Bark does not make a long-lasting path unless, like the gravel, you lay it on top of a plastic sheet. Otherwise it will gradually work its way into the soil underneath. It is, however, relatively cheap and easy to use and can be topped up if necessary.

Gravel, too, if you have not used it elsewhere, makes a good path, although it sticks to the bottom of your shoes and then magically unsticks as soon as you walk into the house. Gravel can be used in combination with other materials – perhaps a few good York paving stones set at regular intervals down the length of the path, surrounded by gravel. It will need some sort of edging to keep it from being scattered over borders and lawns.

Some of the best paths, such as those at Sissinghurst, the National Trust garden in Kent, are made from a random selection of bricks, cobbles and rubble. Some patterning of the materials – using bricks always in threes, incorporating regular roundels made from bits of blue and white china, making parallel lines of cobbles down the sides – gives a better effect than total anarchy.

JOBS FOR THE MONTH

Flowers

❀ Prune late-flowering clematis, those that bear their flowers on new growth made this season. Cut down all stems to about 2ft/60cm above the ground. You will probably have to sacrifice precocious fat buds, but the clematis quickly makes up for lost time.

❀ Winter prune wisteria, finishing off the job you started (or should have) last July. Continue to train in all the growths you want to keep. Cut back the rest of the lateral growths (those springing from the main stem) to two buds. Hard pruning encourages flowering in wisteria, which otherwise produces a mass of leaf. Hot summers also have a marked effect on the following season's performance.

❀ Hard prune late summer flowering shrubs such as buddleja. (In the north or where late frosts are the rule, this job should be left until March.)

❀ Hard prune dogwoods and other shrubs grown for their winter bark. Hard pruning encourages the fresh growth that is more brightly coloured than old stems.

❀ Feed herbaceous borders, spreading well-rotted manure or compost between the plants. If plants need splitting and resetting, do this before you mulch.

❀ Mulch lily of the valley and Solomon's seal with well-rotted compost. Mushroom compost, the waste product of the mushroom-growing industry, is excellent for jobs such as this as it is friable and weed-free.

❀ Prune winter-flowering jasmine as soon as flowers have finished. Take out some of the old, brown wood entirely, making the cut at the base of the plant. This will mean sacrificing some of the new green wood that shoots from the brown, but is the best way to renew the plant. Do not give it an all-over haircut,

which reduces most of the wood that you want to keep.

❧ Start to sow annuals. Use good, fresh compost. Compact it gently before sowing and water it. Spread the seeds as thinly as possible over the surface of the compost. Cover them with a layer of vermiculite – much easier to use than compost as covering. Some very small seeds do not need covering at all. Sprinkle the surface lightly with water and cover with a sheet of paper and a sheet of glass to conserve moisture. Do not let the compost dry out. Remove the coverings when seedlings show signs of germinating and put them in a light place so that growth is not straggly. Prick out seedlings when the first true leaves have developed. Handle them only by the seed leaves, not by the stem. Set the seedlings so that the leaves rest on the surface of the compost. Water lightly and protect from direct sunlight until the seedlings are established.

Vegetables

❧ Plant shallots 6in/15cm apart in rows 9in/23cm apart. Cover them with wire netting if cats or birds are a problem. Once they have rooted, they will be less easy to tweak out and you can remove the netting.

❧ Feed asparagus beds with a general fertilizer.

❧ Lay seed potatoes in shallow trays to sprout before planting.

Fruit

❧ Cut off the tips of raspberry canes, so that they do not wave around above the topmost supporting wire.

❧ Spray peach trees against peach leaf curl, where this is a problem. Providing some sort of overhead cover for trees cuts down the likelihood of infection.

Propagating

❧ Take cuttings of pelargonium and fuchsia.

MARCH

Haircuts and Hatchet Jobs

Clematis to be hard pruned now

'Comtesse de Bouchaud'
C. × durandii
'Ernest Markham'
'Gipsy Queen'
'Gravetye Beauty'
'Huldine'
'Jackmanii Superba'
'Lady Betty Balfour'
'Star of India'
'Ville de Lyon'
All the late-flowering
C. viticella varieties
such as
'Abundance'
'Alba Luxurians'
'Etoile Violette'
'Royal Velours'

A great deal of inadvertent pruning takes place in ferocious winter storms. Sometimes disconsolate rooks flap round our village for days, their rookery having disappeared in one morning's blow. The pigeons seem happy enough with life in the remaining yew trees, but the rooks usually avoid evergreens.

Unfortunately, most storm pruning takes place on those things that I had much rather have been left alone. There is no help with the far more necessary task of cutting back clematis, jasmine, buddleja, caryopteris, roses, all of which need to be done now.

I am not what you might call a natural pruner. I have to be feeling particularly irritable to do a decent job on roses. A good, prolonged bout of irritability rarely comes to order at the right time of year. The job is made more difficult when there is optimistic early growth on shrubs, encouraged by unusually mild weather during winter.

However, with the image of an intractable traffic warden firmly in mind, I shot out recently between the storms and did a hatchet job on the late-flowering clematis. It was not easy. Thick, juicy new growths, more than 6in/15cm long, were already in evidence and I felt like a murderer. I muttered all those questionable phrases you hear in childhood. 'It'll be good for you in the long run,' 'You have to be cruel to be kind.' Despite this, the fact remains that this pruning is more for our benefit than the clematis's. Late clematises flower on new growth and this grows more vigorously on a pruned plant than an unpruned one.

Make the cuts about 18in/45cm above the ground, slicing just above a likely pair of buds. If, as will be the case with a well established clematis, you have five or six stems to deal with, splay them out and tie them in over a wide span, so that as they begin to grow, they will not tangle with each other.

You do not need to be so vicious with the mid-season clematis, those such as 'Mrs Cholmondeley' that start flowering with a great burst in May and June, but drift on towards a second flush in August and September. A minor irritation will do perfectly well for these as they need not so much pruning as thinning. Cut out all the dead growth above the last plump bud or growing shoot. If no more pressing tasks are at hand, fan out the growing stems over their support. To do this you will need to cut all the tendrils that cling to each other so tenaciously, making the top half of the plant as impenetrable as a back-combed hair-do.

Shrub roses present an altogether thornier problem. Reference books suggest they need no pruning, but they can become an overgrown mess. 'Ispahan', a damask rose from the Middle East which bears intensely fragrant semi-double flowers of light pink,

MARCH

Clematis that need light pruning now

'Barbara Jackman'
'Beauty of Worcester'
'Bees' Jubilee'
'Daniel Deronda'
'Elsa Späth'
'Henryi'
'Lady Northcliffe'
'Lasurstern'
'Marcel Moser'
'Marie Boisselot'
'Mrs Cholmondeley'
'Nelly Moser'
'Niobe'
'Perle d'Azur'
'The President'
'Vyvyan Pennell'

is supposed to be a manageable shrub rose, 4ft/1.2m high by 3ft/90cm wide, but some of the growths I dragged out this week were 12ft/3.5m long. It must have its feet in a midden of formidable potency.

Even before the storms, I had decided that something had to be done about this rose. Many of the old shrub roses can discreetly be kept within bounds if you corset them with a couple of strong semicircular iron hoops on long legs. 'Ispahan' was way beyond this treatment and the gales had snapped off some of the lashing growths. The broken ones I pruned out right at the base of the shrub. Then I chose two of the oldest stems (those with the darkest wood) and cut those out altogether as well. It is a huge improvement and gives a little elbow room to the shrubs around.

Each winter now I shall pull out some of the old wood. Though I do not grow them myself, I think, by those that I have seen, that the same treatment would suit some of the bourbon roses, 'Boule de Neige', 'Mme Isaac Pereire' and their like, if they are getting above themselves. Better to remove some of the old wood entirely than give the whole shrub an army haircut.

With the bit now firmly between my teeth, I turned to 'Constance Spry', a modern climbing rose bred by David Austin, with richly scented, pink, cabbagy flowers. Last summer, most of these decorated the sparrows' homes up in the eaves. I untied the rose a branch at a time, cut out one of the oldest stems entirely, shortened the others and tied them in again as horizontal as I could make them in the space. I hope that this will persuade them to decorate my porch rather than the sparrows'.

The very broad rule of thumb for shrubs that flower on new wood is that they are best pruned just as they finish flowering. But pruning has the effect of stimulating new growth, which on late-flowering shrubs would be vulnerable to winter weather. Pruning of late-summer performers which flower on new growth, such as the butterfly bush (*Buddleja davidii*), is therefore best left until now. Buddleja grows at a prodigious rate, so you do not need to be tender with it. Using heavy-duty loppers if necessary, cut back all the previous season's growth to within 2–3in/5–7cm of the old wood. Nothing dire will happen to the buddleja if you do not prune, but flowers may well be less showy than those on an unpruned specimen.

Caryopteris is another late-summer shrub that will need attention in the next few weeks. It is a low-growing plant that bears clusters of soft blue flowers among the pointed grey-green leaves in August and September. Cut out entirely any weak, straggly growths and prune the main framework of the shrub hard back, cutting just above young, healthy buds.

Jasmine, now at the end of its season, is often

subjected to the haircut treatment. Bushes alongside
front doors seem especially prone, all the new growth
reduced to a series of stubby green twigs, laid over a
thick, tangled bird's nest of old, barren brown stems.
Its natural habit, though lanky, is rather more elegant
than this and it is best to arrange it so that the new
green growths can cascade down for their full length.

In any pruning exercise, you need to take account
of the shrub's own personality and not impose your
own too vigorously upon it. A garden is not a parade
ground. With jasmine, the best method is to cut out
some old buff-coloured stems entirely each year.
With these you will also lose some good new green
growths springing from the old. These will quickly
be replaced by new shoots breaking at or near the
base of the plant. Tie these in closely to the wall or
support. As they grow, you can then allow the side
growths breaking from the ribs that you have fanned
out to fall like a curtain in front of the old stems.

I Garden Therefore I am Perfectly Sane

You don't find a lot about gardening in the annals of psychology or psychiatry. Nothing in fact. My own theory about this (you have to have a theory in this line of business) is that the act of gardening itself is what keeps you out of the hands of the shrinks.

I have been looking for an answer to the question: Why do we garden? That is what pitched me into Jung and Freud, Eysenck and theories of identity. I think I'm better off with *Propagation and Planting of the Lesser Saxifragaceae*.

I suppose I never expected Freud to have much of an answer. He is an inside man. Too much sex, too much Vienna to have time for gardeners. I hoped that Jung would be more fertile territory. It seemed entirely possible that the collective unconscious might include gardening among its baggage. But no. A gardener is not an archetype. The very strength of gardening lies in its multiplicity. Each takes from it what he needs. And the needs change.

At the heart of it all, as far as I am concerned, is the feeling that you are abandoning a timetable constructed around dentist's appointments, car ser-vices and the possible arrival of trains, to plunge headlong into a different one, an immense and inexorable one entirely outside your control.

This of course is not a conscious feeling. When I wander out of the back door to do some casual gardening I do not say, 'Fancy that. I am part of the great diurnal round.' I just get on with the weeding. But while you are there, idly looking at the silhouette of the mahonia in the dusk and the sun sets round you, bleeding across the sky with the savage intensity that only happens on winter afternoons, you feel a whole lot better than you do inside. Colder, but better. Or am I a masochist? Too much amateur psychology is bad for you.

This feeling is, to a certain extent, satisfied by a good long country walk. The extra dimension that gardening adds is that you are actively involved in the process. This leads on to two other theories. We garden because we like looking after things (the nurture principle). We garden because we cannot paint or sculpt (the creative principle).

The nurture thing takes people different ways. If you have small children, you don't often have the time, energy or motive to look after much else. If you don't, you have cats or dogs or houseplants. Or you garden. There are very few people who are brave enough not to want anything to need them. Single women garden brilliantly. They can be single-minded about it. Gay men also seem to have a particular gift for gardening.

Nurture does not come high on the list of my own

reasons for gardening (but is this a front?). Perhaps the presence at various stages of three children, dog, several cats, three dozen bantams, herds of guinea pigs and gerbils, two sheep, a rabbit and a trio of goldfish has something to do with that.

I like plants to do well, but I do not take it personally if they decide to die. I am slightly obsessed with feeding things. Does this count as nurture, or is it a conditioned reflex? I seem never to have hit that dewy, straw-hatted stratum of gardening that goes on in magazines. Muck-carting is a more likely pastime than dead-heading.

I am extremely interested in knowing where and how a plant grows in the wild, because that makes it easier to decide where it is likely to thrive in the garden. Once planted, to a great extent, the plant has to fend for itself.

I do very little watering, which is odd, considering the manic desire to feed. Like most gardeners, the first thing I do when I return home from away is to walk round the garden. I do not think this has anything to do with nurturing; more to do with repossession of territory.

Gardeners heavily into nurturing usually choose inherently difficult plants to look after: alpines, miffy dwarf bulbs, orchids. Nurturing them combines with a secret, delicious feeling of superiority, of having conned a saxifrage, tuned to an existence high on a

rocky alpine slope with drainage like a sieve, that it is at home in the damp of a Home Counties greenhouse. There is massive expertise here, but this is plantsmanship, a very particular sort of gardening.

Gardening to me implies more than plants. Inherent in it is the idea of a setting. A gardener makes a sort of dream, a world in his own image – or a world to blot out the image of the real one that lies outside his boundaries.

There are several more motives mixed up here. Foremost is the act of creating the garden, the pleasure of making something, of feeling that your labour alone has transformed a modest square of concrete into something that delights the senses. A good garden delights more senses than any other art. You can smell it, touch it, listen to it, look at it, eat it.

Creating a garden is as valid an artistic experience as anything that Rodin may have felt, bashing away at his sculpture. It is important that tenets of so-called good taste should not intrude here. Gardening must never be put on a pedestal. All that matters is that it should give its maker pleasure.

How you make the garden depends on culture, conditioning, conformity, childhood, compulsion and a clutch of other entries in my ABC of psychology. 'How' is a different question, though. We had better stick to why.

Knitted into the business of making, of creating,

is a sense of escape. In your garden you make the kind of world you wish you lived in. Some gardeners are control freaks. Edging and cutting back and tying in are always to the forefront of their minds. Others drift through a blur of foxglove and wild briar that would drive control freaks round the bend. Some are unsure who they are. The rich among them hire landscape designers to tell them.

Having a choice about why you garden is an indication of relative prosperity. The most pressing reason to do it is to eat. There is dignity, self esteem involved in providing food for a family. A Dorset neighbour takes pride in the fact that his wife, in forty years of marriage, has never had to buy a vegetable. She of course may secretly be longing to splash out on a sinful aubergine or a self-indulgent snack of baby sweetcorn. If so, it doesn't show.

In Candide's best of possible worlds, we would not garden to outdo our neighbours. Competitiveness has a place on the show bench among giant onions, marrows and vases of sweet peas. It should not be apparent in gardens themselves, although of course it is.

It is particularly prevalent among those who open their gardens for the National Gardens Scheme. Success is measured in numbers of visitors rather than anything else. It is bad enough having this sort of game played endlessly round your children ('And *how* many GCSEs did you say?'). Intolerable to have your confidence as a gardener undermined as well as your competence as a parent. There are, of course, people who do not garden at all, though such deprivation is too awful to contemplate.

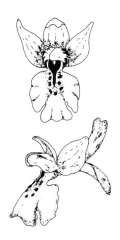

HAUGHTY HYBRIDS

I confess I have always been intimidated by orchids. They seem to look at me in the supercilious way that camels do, noting imperfections of dress and appearance and comparing them unfavourably with their own statuesque flawlessness.

I tried to pretend that I did not like orchids, but this was not true. I like them very much indeed. The problem lay in my awe of them. I could not see these highly bred aristocrats sharing the kitchen table with yogurt pots, newspapers, coffee mugs and all the other mundane detritus of family life.

Ray Bilton assures me that I am wrong. Ray is a great orchid man and owner of the famous McBeans nursery in Sussex, where orchids have been grown for more than a hundred years. Everything you will read here I have learned from Ray. It says a great deal for his enthusiasm (and his salesmanship) that I came away from the nursery clutching, not too gingerly, a splendid phalaenopsis orchid called 'Brighton Belle'.

It is the colour of a cyclamen, with a long wiry

stem rising about 3ft/90cm from six long boat-shaped leaves at the base. There are three blooms out and eleven more to come. I have had it a whole week and it has not died yet. My confidence is increasing in leaps and bounds.

They are used to novices at McBeans and send each probationer away with a small postcard-sized set of instructions. I learned that phalaenopsis grow naturally in the Philippines where they are epiphytic, which is to say that they grow on other plants without actually being parasitic, and frequently produce aerial roots.

McBeans' marketing manager Michael Tibbs, also a passionate orchid grower, spends a good deal of time in the jungles where orchids grow, studying and photographing them – and living with them. 'A person can only grow orchids, understand how they evolve, by living like an orchid,' he says. 'We grow only hybrids. The original species are always left in the jungles where they grow naturally.'

In their natural habitat they are used to higher levels of humidity than we get in Britain and so will be happiest standing on a tray of damp gravel. Plants should never be allowed to dry out completely, but on the other hand the compost should never be waterlogged. Ray Bilton suggests standing the pot on the draining board and dribbling a pint of water through it once a week.

Every other week from March to August you need to add a liquid feed such as Fisons Liquinure mixed at half strength. During September and October, when the plants are building up to their main flowering period, you should switch to a feed high in potash, such as Fisons Tomorite. It was comforting to think that orchids and tomatoes had some needs in common.

Where I am likely to fall down is in the matter of room temperature. As we do not have central heating, it is only in the Aga-warmed kitchen that we can get anywhere near the orchid's minimum winter temperature of 60°F/15°C. The best day temperature is said to be around 70°F/21°C. Orchids do not like direct sunlight, which is fine because there is not a lot of that here either.

The phalaenopsis orchids are not what Ray Bilton's nursery is best known for. Cymbidiums and odontoglossums are their speciality. The odontoglossums look fiendishly difficult. 'Not difficult, challenging,' said Mr Bilton reprovingly. He is what they call a positive thinker. Odontoglossums come from Central or South America and in the wild grow at very high altitudes. When they started to come into England at the end of the nineteenth century, enthusiasts paid a thousand pounds for a single plant.

Ray Bilton started a complex hybridizing programme with his odontoglossums which gave him

35,000 unnamed seedlings. All these were grown up to flowering size and then he selected a few that he thought worthy of christening. He has very high standards.

Hybridizing is his passion, but the whole programme took a pitiful battering in the 1987 hurricane, which smashed several of his glasshouses to bits. Thousands of plants were cut to ribbons by flying glass, others were hurled to the floor where leaves were bruised and battered. In the damaged houses, 70 per cent of his plants were destroyed. Some hybrids, although damaged, he kept because they were vital to his breeding programme.

All the plants begin life in the laboratory of the nursery. Possible new hybrids start from seeds sown in a sterile gel which is then sealed in milk bottles. Established clones are mass-produced by micropropagation and these tiny scraps of tissue also start life in milk-bottle propagators. There is a whole room full of them, laid like wine bottles on their sides in racks round the room. A piece of tissue started off in gel today would take four years to grow into a saleable flowering plant.

The technique of micropropagation has had a marked effect on the price of orchids. Many of the plants in McBeans' catalogue can be had for £15. They were charging 15 guineas for a plant in a magnificent 1922 catalogue that Ray still has. That was

ten weeks' wages for his father, a Durham coalminer.

Orchids were expensive because they used to be very difficult to propagate from seed. Then some observant person noticed that in the wild any surviving seedlings usually sprang up close to the mother plant. It turned out that a fungus in the roots of the mother plant was an essential catalyst in the seeds' germination.

By 1926 an American, Professor Knudson, was showing propagators at McBeans how to innoculate their sowing medium with the nutrients provided by the fungus. For the next forty years more than a million seedlings were successfully raised by this method until in 1964 another don, Professor Morel, trained Ray Bilton in the revolutionary technique of propagation by tissue culture.

New hybrids can only be produced from seed, and it is the restless pursuit of an ideal hybrid that keeps Ray Bilton shut up in his repaired glasshouses week after week. Present glories interest him less than future possibilities. His favourite hybrid will always be the one that exists only in his mind.

NOVICE GARDENERS: PART THREE
Giving Edge to your Backyard

Verticals in a garden have the disconcerting habit of
suddenly transforming themselves into horizontals.
The most important part of a vertical is the bit that
you cannot see, the bit that is under the ground,
securing (you hope) and anchoring the structure.
Garden boundaries account for most of the headaches
in vertical gardening, for they are essential. The rest
is trimmings. The first thing to sort out is which of
your boundaries are your responsibility and which
your neighbours'. Local papers are full of the high
dramas that erupt if you get it wrong. 'Neighbour's
fence frenzy', 'Boundary breaking point'. Only rows
and resignations in the local operatic society com-
mand more column inches. Even if you are certain
of your rights of ownership, it is sensible to talk to
your neighbour before starting any major upheaval.
Someone has to look at the other side of whatever
structure you are proposing to put up.

High boundaries seem an advantage when you are
hemmed in by things that you would rather not see
and, at the same time, lacking any place where the
neighbours cannot see you. Height of boundaries
must be considered in relation to the overall size of
the garden. A small patch will become a claustropho-
bic prison if surrounded on all sides by tall walls and

fences. You should also consider shadows. The taller a boundary, the longer these will be. A great many people see their gardens only at the beginning and the end of each day, when the sun is low in the sky and the shadows naturally at their longest. Tall fences will only exacerbate this problem. An illusion of privacy can be given by keeping the general level of the fence at medium height, but with a few high points built in. These can be iron hoops or trellis arches or simple pole structures to carry climbers up and beyond the general boundary horizon.

Very few people move into a house with no boundary markers whatsoever. The luckiest will have brick or stone walls to work with. In sub-basement flats, brick walls may seem overpowering, but can be transformed if they are painted. White is often the first thought because it brings light into an area. Conversely, it looks grubby more quickly than any other colour and is not as natural in our soft light as it is in the blinding light of the Mediterranean. Try instead buffs and creams, perhaps sponged over with pinks and browns to give a mottled marbled effect. This works as well outside as it does in and makes a particularly good background for dramatic foliage plants.

Trompe-l'oeil paintings on vertical surfaces are vogueish, but, like most jokes, only work once. I suspect they would be tiresomely self-conscious things to live with. Mirrors have greater possibilities in bringing about the same end – that is, to make the garden appear larger than it is. Mirrors must be used unobtrusively, not blatantly; the edges must be well disguised, so that you are not quite sure where reality ends and illusion begins. You do not have to go to the expense of buying properly mirrored plate glass. A sheet of aluminium foil sealed behind a piece of ordinary glass will give the right slightly distorted effect.

Mirror can also be used to suggest panelled doors let in to side boundaries of brick. The panelled frame gives extra height within the boundary and the mirror glass set in the panels reflects the greenery of your own garden, but gives the illusion that you are actually looking through the door into some unknown ground beyond. All such tricksy effects need to be well masked with swags of wisteria or ivy or fig, or such a door will just look as if it has been left behind by an absent-minded builder.

New houses often have boundaries of uncompromising chain link fencing which makes the garden feel like an outpost of Stalag Luft III. It must be disguised, but planting a hedge to screen it takes up valuable space. Think instead of constructing some form of simple arbour alongside your chain link fence. Larch poles are good for longevity, but any structurally sound timber will do. Four or five uprights joined

by poles along the top is all that is needed. Plant these with climbers, using plenty of leafy subjects such as vines, mixed up with the roses, clematis and honeysuckle. Keep them well trained in, twisting new growths around the uprights and along the top poles. Meanwhile, plant ivy at 2ft/60cm intervals along the chain link fence. It will gradually climb and cover the fence and make a handsome green backdrop for foreground planting. When the fence is fully covered, you can snip off any growths that start questing sideways towards the wooden poles.

Hedges are now an unpopular option for boundaries. They take up sideways space, unless they are rigorously controlled, and need regular clipping. The ones that need the least clipping are also the slowest. Hedges should not be entirely discounted, however, particularly for boundaries alongside roads. They filter wind effectively, and are more difficult to get up and over than walls or fences. A thorn hedge, properly maintained, provides the most impenetrable barrier of all – dog-, child- and vandal-proof. A hedge also softens the outlook round a garden in which there are already lots of hard materials – perhaps a concrete path, paved terrace, tarmac drive – and is valuable for the texture that it contributes in a largely man-made environment. Beech, hornbeam and thorn all make solid hedges. Holly, box and yew are additionally evergreen, but are much slower.

Wood panelling of various kinds is one of the most popular options, because it is a quick and relatively cheap way of solving the boundary problem. It also has a great deal of built-in wind resistance. For all types of wood fencing, use the heftiest fencing posts you can afford, for they are no more trouble to set into the ground than the more flimsy ones and may save much aggravation when the equinoctial gales start to blow. Most modern fenceposts will have been pressure-injected with fungicide, which greatly extends their life. They will still need an annual coat of preservative, which is a bore when they are all nicely swathed with climbers.

Wattle fencing, woven willow and hazel hurdles are more attractive to look at, but can only be considered as temporary stopgaps. They are excellent for internal divisions of a garden, perhaps separating vegetable plot from flowers, or providing a screen round a hard-surfaced area of compost bins and wheelbarrows. Each screen gives you an extra opportunity to grow climbers or make a support for sweet peas or nasturtiums.

Fancier divisions can be dreamed up in trellis work, or 'treillage' as it is known in smart circles. The chief problem, it seems to me, is getting the rest of the garden to live up to it. Painted white, it is extremely dominant. Painted dark green, it is more recessive, but will swallow up the outlines of similarly green

71

leaves – although variegated foliage will look well displayed against it.

The most important rules are scale and fitness for purpose. It is senseless to construct a grand processional way of trellis through the garden if it only leads to the rubbish dump. Resist the urge to be over-complicated. Too many swoops and curves in the outline will lead to seasickness. One of the most pleasant ways of using trellis is as a surround for a seat – back, sides and perhaps a pointed roof. Make it strong so that it will bear the weight of a climbing rose such as 'Seagull' or 'Wedding Day'. Then you can view the world serenely through a cascade of sweetly scented blossom. For a short time, at least.

JOBS FOR THE MONTH

General

❀ Treat drives, paths and paved areas with a residual weedkiller containing simazine, atrazine or dichlobenil. Used carefully, these are great allies.

❀ Spring-clean houseplants, taking off dead leaves and dusting over the foliage with either a damp sponge or a leaf wipe. All houseplants will now need more food and water. Those that seem to be bursting out of their containers may need repotting. Do not suppose that, by giving it a pot twice as big, a plant will be twice as happy. One size larger will be plenty.

❀ Moss often has a field day in lawns through the winter. If you cannot learn to love it, hire a scarifier and sweat a weekend away tearing the stuff out of your lawn. A chemical mosskiller is a lazier option.

Flowers

❀ Prune hybrid tea roses and climbers that flower on the current season's growth. (In mild areas, this is a job that can be done in January and February.)

❀ Cut fuchsia and mallow stems back to live wood.

❀ Pull any dead leaves away from the rhizomes of bearded iris and give them a feed of bonemeal. If you are lucky enough to have flowers of *Iris unguicularis*, keep picking them. They will fare much better indoors than out.

❀ Plant acidantheras and anemones.

❀ Set begonia tubers in boxes of peat. As soon as they have sprouted, plant them out in separate pots.

❀ Start overhauling herbaceous borders, lifting and dividing congested clumps of plants and replanting them in soil enriched with compost and bonemeal. Michaelmas daisy, rudbeckia and phlox especially benefit from this treatment. As they age, growth tends to die out in the centre of the clumps. The most vigorous growth is usually round the edges: these are the pieces that you should choose for replanting.

❀ Late-summer shrubs that bear their flowers on this season's growth (buddleja, caryopteris etc) should be cut hard back now. If you have inherited a really overgrown buddleja, bring it to heel gradually, by cutting out half the stems this season, half next. Flowers are larger on hard-pruned specimens than on those left to their own devices.

❀ Choose some hardy annuals for sowing directly into the ground where they are to flower.

🌺 Plant gladioli, setting the corms 4–6in/10–15cm deep in well-drained soil in full sun.

🌺 Lift and split clumps of snowdrops and aconites if you want to hasten their spread through the garden. Replant them with a generous portion of bonemeal mixed into the earth. Snowdrops settle far more successfully 'in the green' than as dry bulbs.

Vegetables

🌺 Sow parsnips in drills about ½in/12mm deep in rows 12in/30cm apart.

🌺 Sow summer spinach in drills ½in/12mm deep, the rows 12in/30cm apart. It will do best in a half-shaded spot where there is rich, moist soil. In drought conditions it runs quickly to seed. Some varieties such as 'Norvak' have good resistance to bolting.

🌺 Sow broad beans if the ground is not too wet. Take out a shallow drill about 12in/30cm wide and sow the beans in a broad band so that when they are grown, they give each other some support.

🌺 Sow celery and celeriac indoors, scattering the seed thinly over the compost. Celery is a hefty feeder, so if the ground is workable, start to prepare the patch outside with a layer of manure in the bottom of a 12in/30cm deep trench.

🌺 Sow carrots.

🌺 Sow leeks in a seed bed for transplanting later on.

🌺 Sow Brussels sprouts if you need masses. If you do not, it is simpler to buy a dozen plants later in the season.

Fruit

🌺 Mulch currants and gooseberries thickly to keep down weeds and conserve moisture.

🌺 Perfectionists should spray apple and pear trees against scab using Benlate or Dithane, if no more pressing tasks are to hand. Scab is a blemish rather than a threat. Trees will not die from it.

Propagating

🌺 Divide aconitum, aster, astilbe, chrysanthemum, dicentra, echinops, geum, helenium, hosta, inula, lamium, libertia, ligularia, liriope, lysichiton, lysimachia, mint, osmunda, phlox, rodgersia, sisyrinchium, solidago, thalictrum.

🌺 Take hardwood cuttings of eucryphia and willow.

🌺 Set rooted cuttings of tender perennials such as penstemon and semi-tender shrubs such as argyranthemum and artemisia into individual small pots.

🌺 Start feeding rooted cuttings of heather.

APRIL

First Cut the Corner off your Seed Packet

To the uninitiated, seed sowing is the impenetrable rite of passage that separates the novice from the seasoned gardener. Like having babies, it is not usually half as difficult as experts try to make it. Nor do you need great batteries of equipment. Propagator heat makes plants grow faster than they would otherwise do, but at some stage they must learn to do without it and take on the weather as it really is, nasty, brutish and worse than they thought. The tougher they have been raised, the better they will be able to cope.

All the seeds I have sown this year were raised on the kitchen windowsill, where the temperature is at most 60°F/15°C. Once pricked out into seed trays, the seedlings move into the sitting room, where there is a very convenient long windowsill, north-facing, that takes ten seed trays, resting on wads of newspaper, with aluminium foil underneath to stop the damp seeping through to the woodwork.

The temperature here, farthest from the open fire that provides the only heating, is a chillier 55°F/13°C actually slightly cooler than the cold frame outside. When they go out there, it won't be too much of a shock. I might join them, having just discovered with the aid of my speedy digital thermometer that they will be rather warmer outside than I am inside.

Ageratum, asters, bupleurum, echium, erigeron, lobelia, phlox, rhodochiton and statice are some of the seedlings that are waiting to go out. It is still not too late to sow. If you have never tried raising seed before, take the plunge now, choosing flowers that germinate fairly quickly like alyssum, English or French marigolds, cosmos, godetia or petunia.

The magazine *Gardening from Which?* carried out some interesting experiments in the north of England which showed that late-sown seed often caught up with early hopefuls. Asters sown in the first week of May, for instance, flowered at exactly the same time (the third week in August) as those sown a month earlier.

So, hanging on to the fact that seeds are strongly programmed for survival, and will desperately try to do the right thing even if you are doing the wrong, buy a packet and see what happens. Make things easier for yourself by avoiding seeds that have compli-cated escape mechanisms. Fast-growing cosmos is one of the prettiest of the bomb-proof annuals. It has delicate feathery foliage, grows about 3ft/90cm high, thrives on poor thin soils such as you often find in town gardens, and has large daisy flowers in various shades of deep pink and white. They will go on until the first frosts of autumn.

Save your seed trays until a later stage in the

APRIL

proceedings and use a clean plastic pot about 5in/ 13cm across for the initial sowing of seed. Fill it with compost and firm it down gently. Scatter the seed as thinly and evenly as you can over the surface of the compost, then cover it with a thin layer of vermiculite.

This is very much easier to use as a seed covering than compost, as it drains quickly. You do not have to worry about the exact depth of the covering as you do if you are using compost. Water the pot thoroughly before sealing it up in a cocoon of clingfilm, which will prevent the compost drying out.

Many flowers, such as nemesia, pansy and verbena, germinate best in total darkness, so you can shut the whole pot in an airing cupboard, if you like quick results, or cover the pot on a windowsill with a piece of card or a wadge of newspaper.

Some seed does best in light. Do not cover up ageratum, alyssum, snapdragon, lobelia, mimulus, impatiens, nicotiana or petunia. Cosmos seed can be covered up, but watch for emerging seedlings after a week. They usually germinate in about seven to fourteen days. French marigolds are even quicker. Sometimes they are up in two days. You need to whip the coverings off them as soon as they are properly through, before they bump their heads against the covering and start to bend like Atlas, with the weight of the world on their wobbly shoulders.

Once they have germinated, you need to move seedlings on to fresh quarters sooner rather than later. Growing close together, as they do in the initial seed pot, seedlings quickly get leggy, too much stem to top, and then they keel over at the slightest disturbance.

You also need to water them as the compost begins to dry out. They do not need a permanent bog round them, however. If you are growing on a windowsill, you will need to turn the pots round regularly, as the seedlings always tip themselves towards the light.

One evening when you feel in need of some calmingly therapeutic activity, fill some full-sized seed trays with compost, gently firm down the surface and with your forefinger, poke a grid of holes in the compost, seven along the long side, four along the short.

With a lolly stick, the handle of a teaspoon, or whatever you find comfortable, gently ease up a few seedlings at a time from the pot. Pick each one up by a leaf and drop it by turn into the holes you have made in the compost in the seed tray. Set them deep so that the first pair of leaves sits on the surface of the compost. Firm the compost round them gently with your fingers. When the whole tray is planted, water it thoroughly with a fine-nozzled can.

The compost should contain enough food for the seedlings to live on until they are planted out towards the end of May. Watering will be the most important

APRIL

job, then getting the plants acclimatized to the real world. Do this gently, putting the trays out on warm-ish days and bringing them in at nights, until the plants seem sturdy enough to be planted out. When they are, you will find they have a magnetic attrac-tion – not only for you but for children, footballs and dogs as well. Small children have a consuming interest in how the roots of things are coming along. No gismo has yet been invented to get over that problem.

⊷⊗⊶

ALPINE PEAKS

'In some odd corner you rigged up a dump of broken cement blocks, and added bits of stone and fragments of statuary. You called this "The Rockery" and proudly led your friends to see it, and planted it all over with Periwinkle to hide the hollows in which your Alpines had promptly died.' Reginald Farrer, father of the twentieth-century rock garden, wrote this in 1913, but it still has a ghastly relevance today. Nothing you can do to builders' rubble will ever make it look like an alpine scree. A breeze block is a breeze block, however sweetly set around with cushions of saxifrage.

This is not to say that we should do without alpine plants, but that we should perhaps abandon attempts to build the Alps as well. Even stone specially bought in from the garden centre cannot magically transmute itself into a landscape feature as it is tipped from the lorry. The sort of stones that you can shift about without ending up in an orthopaedic ward are usually too small to build a natural-looking rock outcrop. You end up with a currant bun instead.

There are other ways of doing things. Provided you always keep in mind the sort of conditions that alpine plants thrive in, you can grow them in many different places in the garden: in the cracks between paving stones on terraces and paths, in raised beds and cavity walls, in lawns and screes, in shallow troughs and pans and in cool greenhouses.

In any of these situations, the key to success is good drainage. Use the modified compost you can buy at specialist nurseries such as Ingwersen's, or make up your own, adding extra grit to a loam-based mixture. Gravel chippings are also invaluable. They make a fast-draining layer round the necks of alpine plants, and prevent rot. They keep down weeds and cut down on the amount of watering you have to do in the summer.

Troughs and pans provide one of the most enter-taining ways of growing alpines. They are grown-up versions of the children's 'garden on a plate' compe-titions you see at horticultural shows. Stone troughs made their first appearance at Chelsea in the mid-

APRIL

twenties, planted up by Clarence Elliott of the famed Six Hills nursery.

They are more difficult to find now, and expensive, but you can make DIY versions with two cardboard boxes, one smaller than the other, to provide a mould. Fill the gap between the boxes with a mixture of sand (one part), cement (one part) and dry peat (two parts), made into a stiff porridge with a little water. When this fake stone has set, you can liberate it from its cardboard mould. The same mix will disguise white glazed sinks, very much cheaper to buy than the stone ones. Score the slippery surface with a chisel and use epoxy resin to help the mixture stick as you slap it on.

Spring is the peak of the year for alpine plants, and the sort of bulbs that fit very well with them: fritillaries, scillas, dwarf narcissus and species tulips. When you are planting a pan or trough you need also to include one or two plants that will peak later on in the year – rock phloxes or miniature pinks.

Fortunately many of the spring-flowering plants such as saxifrages are pleasing enough in form and leaf to pay their way the whole year through. The greyish silvery-edged saxifrages are an excellent foil for early *Iris reticulata* – blue or purple. Keep to the slow-growing kinds and save the more rampageous mossy saxifrages for positions at the front of a border.

This is a huge and diverse family, the sort of challenge that can bring a dangerous gleam into a collector's eye. 'Southside Seedling' has showy rosettes and pink flowers in early summer; 'Whitehill' neat greyish-green rosettes, the back of each leaf stained with red. Like many Kabschia and Euaizoonia types, it has silvery frosting on the edges of the leaves. The white flowers usually appear in April and May.

Dwarf gypsophilas, such as G. *fratensis*, are useful for early summer flowers. These are pink, but the plant is deciduous, so there's a gap in the winter. It droops elegantly. Use it where it can fall over the edge of a container. It will do the same sort of thing in a retaining wall. It is more prostrate than the similar G. *repens*.

Although in a trough you may be gardening in a space no more than 18in/45cm square, it is no less important here than anywhere else to put together plants that set each other off, rather than fight. A few uprights will be needed among the creeping forms, a few neatly sculptural miniature shrubs, such as the slow-growing 'Boughton Dome', a useful evergreen hebe with grey-green leaves and opalescent flowers in the summer. I have yet to learn to love dwarf conifers, but that is probably less the plants' fault than the way they are often used, rising glumly from a dusty tide of heather.

A saxifrage, the domed hebe, the gypsophila, one of the alpine phloxes, such as P. *douglasii* with lilac

APRIL

flowers in early summer or the later-flowering 'Chata-hoochee', a succulent lewisia (horribly susceptible to winter rot) and a shrubby penstemon such as *P. scouleri* would be plenty enough to start a miniature garden. This kind of myopic horticulture is a wonderful time-waster. The less space you have, the more concentrated your eye is, and the more offensive any blemish becomes.

I have been resetting a pan of sempervivums, which were rather graphically showing up the fact that I had not given sufficient attention to drainage in their container – a shallow rectangular terracotta pan. Cleaned of their rotting leaves, the sempervivums are now sitting on top of a deep layer of crocks, covered with fresh compost and a thick dressing of chips. Sempervivums are quiet plants but the symmetry of their form and the stoicism of their nature is impressive. They never flag in a great summer cook-out, while alpines in the troughs shriek with anguish.

Watering troughs is a nightmare, as there is usually no freeboard between the top of the compost and the edge of the trough. Water runs off sooner than soak in. A funnel sunk in the earth proves the easiest way to get the wet where it is most needed.

I have also been fiddling with the half-dozen auricula plants which until last week were still sitting in the plastic drinking cups in which they were given to me last summer on an allotment in Lancashire. Auriculas are strange plants, members of the diverse family of primulas, with a history that binds them strongly to mill towns and mines.

They have fleshy leaves, sometimes thickly dusted with flour, and flowers, coming out now, of weird purple, brown, mustard or red. The more compli-cated show types are even more bizarre with flowers that can be grey or green, or have four concentric circles of colour round a central eye.

They are one of the select band of flowers known as 'florists' flowers' – nothing to do with shops or flower arrangements. The florists were highly com-petitive groups of growers, more common in the industrial north than the south, who emerged in the eighteenth and nineteenth centuries. They grew auriculas, tulips, pinks and one or two other special flowers, and showed them at florists' feasts where enormous prizes changed hands.

Though the old florists' societies don't exist now in that form, auriculas themselves have never lost their appeal. Teachers and engineers are especially susceptible, say Derek and Pamela Salt of Donington Plants in Lincolnshire, if the cross-section of their customers is anything to go by. My half-dozen plants are all show auriculas, including the old variety 'Remus', a blue self, bright 'Red Gauntlet' and dark 'Consett' with particularly good foliage. Now they are all in traditional straight-sided clay pots, which set them off well and reduce the danger of over-watering. Show varieties, particularly any with thickly floured leaves, need shelter from the rain.

The Salts specialize in auriculas and recommend the alpine types as the easiest to grow. They have established several big clumps in a scree bed outside one of the cool greenhouses where the bulk of the plants are kept. For growing outside, they recommend plum-purple 'Argus', the paler 'Lisa' and perhaps a showy double such as 'Doublet'.

Before they started their nursery, Derek Salt looked after the labs at pbi (Pan Britannica Industries), the garden chemical company, and Pamela was agony aunt for *Practical Gardening* magazine. Not too many agonies with auriculas, she says. The chief danger is overwatering in winter, the chief enemy, the dreaded vine weevil. Gamma-HCH (Murphy Gamma BHC Dust) mixed in the compost is the best deterrent. They grow their plants in a free-draining mixture made from two parts of loam, two of peat and one of grit. During the summer, they are fed with Phostrogen, tomato food or whatever else is to hand. Apart from that, they say, there is little to do but enjoy them.

A Room with a View

The garden is perhaps not the first thing you think of each morning, but it may well be the first thing you see – along with the imperfections in the ceiling decor and the pile of books the literary critics say you ought to be reading. The view from the bed may seem a slothful sort of subject for a gardening writer, but it has been in the forefront of my mind recently as my waking view is about to change.

Prominent to the left of it is a bulwark of spotty laurel (*Aucuba japonica*), at the moment conspicuously scattered with fat red berries. This is the only remnant of a Victorian shrubbery planted in front of the house and which we left untouched for years because the children were particularly fond of it. Each had a separate camp there and each held frequent 'At Homes' for the others. The journey from one to the next was no more than a few minutes' crawling, but this did not prevent the visits from being intensely formal affairs.

The visitors perched on upturned logs and sipped potions, made from primroses and mashed leaves, out of old fishpaste jars dug up in the undergrowth. It prepared their stomachs wonderfully well for later onslaughts on pizza parlours and fast-fried chicken joints.

When the clearing began, we planted a winter-flowering cherry, *Prunus subhirtella* 'Autumnalis', to the right of the spotty laurel. This was done entirely without thought as to how it would look from inside, but as the tree grew it filled the centre background view from the bed exactly and has turned out to be the greatest antidote to winter gloom yet invented.

It starts blooming in November and carries on until February, never plastered with flowers but always showing enough of them to lift the spirits and prevent that desire, sometimes overwhelming on winter mornings, to dive under the duvet and stay hidden until spring.

Carried away with this newly discovered insight into the pleasures of gardening from the horizontal, we planted a viburnum in front of the cherry. It was *Viburnum* × *bodnantense* 'Dawn', also a good winter doer with clusters of sweet-smelling flowers from November until March. Sometimes it starts to bloom before the leaves drop, which is a mistake, as the flowers are somehow swallowed up in the foliage. The growth is gaunt and upright but this is an advantage, for low-spreading shrubs such as the variegated *Cotoneaster horizontalis* nearby cannot be seen from the bed.

The land outside the bedroom window rises slightly, which is a good thing for the view from the bed. You see more than if the land were flat. If it falls away, you may catch only the tops of the tallest bushes. This is something you cannot change, but you can perhaps plant climbers instead to poke in round the edges of the windows.

An ancient red rose was already planted near our window so that its new growth fell into the right-hand side of the window frame. I planted 'Constance Spry' on the other side, properly a shrub rose but with growths as long and whippy as any climber. One long stem can usually be tied in under the window sill. Bent horizontal like this, new shoots break out all along the stem so that in July there is a whole row of blowzy pink roses ranged along the sill, agreeable early morning companions as they look good and say nothing.

Clematis 'Jackmanii Superba' was supposed to add to the effect, but the growths are not quite as biddable as the rose's. Before you notice what is happening, a shoot has accelerated away and joined forces with another shrub quite different from the host you had in mind. So many tendrils have in the meanwhile coiled tight to help it on its way, it seems hard to start on corrective training.

The exact position of the new bed in the new bedroom has yet to be decided, but I fancy it will depend more on the view than on the handiness of electric power points. This time the garden will be seen obliquely, rather than head-on. The oblique view is longer, of course. By great good fortune, the

cherry tree is still in the frame, but seen with different companions. The rooks are still there too, wheeling above the trees in the dawn like small lost pieces of the night.

Something bold is called for in the middle distance of the view, where individual blossoms become too distant to make an impact. Perhaps a spire of holly or a purple-leaved pittosporum would be the thing.

The foreground is already in place, indeed has been blooming for a dozen years unseen, at least from this angle, for the room has never yet been occupied. To the left is the wayward but unparalleled ceanothus 'Trewithen Blue', a phenomenal grower but not reliably hardy. In April it is the best thing in the garden and is often in flower from Christmas onwards.

It likes to live dangerously, but nearly came a cropper in one bad winter, when it was struck down, foolishly flowering itself silly. The colour is a mid sky blue, excellent against the large glossy leaves. I am looking forward to waking to that each morning in spring. As there has been no one in the room to notice the fact, a branch has spread right across the window. There is still plenty of light coming in so it will probably be left until it gets cut back, as it will be, by frost.

In a city flat, the view may be composed entirely of elements outside your control: other people's chimneys, an advertisement hoarding, a few branches of a street tree. In these circumstances there is little you can do, except hope the council has run out of money for tree surgery and indulge in a windowbox. If you have casement windows that open out, as they mostly do, a windowbox will have to be mounted too low for you to get much advantage of it from a prone position.

Sash windows, although draughty, are much more accommodating to gardeners. In choosing flowers for windowboxes, avoid varieties with long stems. Stems are unattractive at close quarters and tall flowers are more likely to snap in turbulent winds. For spring, tulips are unparalleled. If you plant Greigii or Fosteriana varieties, you have the added bonus of good foliage, striped and mottled in purplish brown.

NOVICE GARDENERS: PART FOUR
Tripping Out on the Terrace

'The patio' is a term used by estate agents to describe any collection of paving stones loosely attached to a house. Builders like patios because they give an illusion of order to a new house. They push all the muck they should never be leaving behind into a raft around the back door and then drop concrete slabs on top as they retreat off the site – usually for ever.

Gradually the forces of gravity try to make sense of

the plastic sacks, copies of the *Sun*, solidified cement powder, off-cuts of rafters and fossilized sandwiches. The patio begins to heave like the sea in the Bay of Biscay. This is when the novice gardener usually moves in, fired with enthusiasm by articles on making the garden an extension of the living room. There are visions of candlelit supper tables, parasols and loungers. The reality is stubbed toes and chairs that never sit with four legs on the ground.

Patios are like icebergs. What is underneath is more important than what is on top. There is little you can do to disguise the problems of an erupting patio. However much you may try to persuade yourself otherwise, the only true solution is to lift off the top layer and sort out the substratum.

At this point, we veer dangerously near the realms of DIY. The language of tamping beams, plate vibrators, shutter boards, arrissing trowels and the like is music to many people's ears, but not to mine. For those who are happy to go down the DIY road, the simplest guide is *Pave It* by Dek Messecar. If you call in someone else to build or rebuild your patio, make sure the specifications are clear on a few key points. The foundation should be made of 4in/100mm of hardcore, topped up with sand and shingle to give a decent smooth bed for the final layer of paving stones, bricks or whatever material you decide on. The finished level of the patio must be at least 6in/150mm

below the damp course. If this is impossible, plan for a gap of 3in/75mm between terrace and house wall to fill with hardcore topped with pebbles or gravel.

Drainage is another nightmare. Any water that collects on the patio must be persuaded to spill harm-lessly over the garden edge and not in through the kitchen door. House drains and air bricks must also be treated with caution and not immured carelessly behind half a ton of concrete.

The texture of the finished terrace will have an important effect on the pleasure you get from the garden as a whole. Concrete is cheap but, unless used carefully, looks it. Coloured concrete compounds rather than alleviates the inherent deficiencies of the material. A chequerboard of pink, grey and green slabs may seem an interesting idea on paper, but it is an uncompromising pattern to live with. Better to let the colour come from the plants and containers. These can change from season to season and will be shown off far better in a plain setting than against a psychedelic array of chemical dyes.

I would go for a neutral colour, but choose paving slabs with some surface texture. Manufacturers call them riven slabs. Although they do not weather like stone, they are far more pleasing on the eye than the flat, matt surfaces of the standard concrete slab.

Whatever material you use for paving a terrace, it should fit in with the other materials around it. For centuries nobody needed to think about whether it did or not, for buildings grew out of the materials that were most easily to hand. In the Cotswolds it was creamy stone. In Sussex and Kent, where stone was scarce but clay abundant, brick was the natural building material. Among the oak forests of Here-fordshire and the West Midlands, timber-framed houses were the norm. Many of London's terraced houses are built from the same yellowish stock brick. These different colours and textures need to be firmly in your mind when you are thinking about paving.

Brick itself makes a satisfactory surface for terraces, not only because it is full of texture, but because it can be laid in so many different patterns. You could do a whole terrace in basket weave or herringbone, or divide the space into squares with straight double lines of brick, infilling the spaces with bricks laid in a different pattern. They must be frost-proof.

Timber decking has never caught on here in the same way as in the States, where it is often used as a transition between house and garden. I have not tried it in my own garden, but the possibilities are intriguing. Wood is not as durable as concrete or brick, but it has a warm, pleasant texture and is a more malleable material than either of the others.

If I were making a terrace at the moment I would be tempted to experiment with some pleasing bleached greyish wood imported from Canada by the

Longlife Company of Wetherby. I have seen it made up into planked decking, finished with a simple balustrade and wide shallow wooden steps, and there were tables and chairs of the same wood. The whole effect was solid and comforting. The wood is treated with preservative and is beautifully finished.

Timber decking provides a good way of creating a flat space on sloping ground without all the expense of levelling or building up that a concrete terrace would demand on such a site. The deck can sit on a timber underpinning and the supports could easily be clothed with climbers which would then poke their noses in at the level of the decking. Wood gets slippery in wet weather, but there are anti-slither products available.

The amount of space that a patio takes up should bear some reasonable relationship to the size and shape of the garden as a whole. It is more common to make patios too small than too big. You cannot relax in a space if you have to jump out of your chair every time someone else wants to get by.

Do not feel you have to sacrifice garden to terrace. The one can be brought to the other, using big containers. Wooden half barrels are excellent value and the wood, already splendidly pickled in alcohol, is more resistant to rot than you would suppose. Bulk is important in planting containers, particularly if the patio is made of an arid material such as plain

APRIL

95

concrete, butted up against a rendered concrete house wall. Foliage, preferably evergreen, will do more to soften the scene than any number of petunias or geraniums.

I always used to look for colour in whatever I was planting in my pots. At the moment, I do things the other way around. I have been collecting highly glazed pots, usually Chinese because they are the cheapest, and planting them with more restrained plants. My most recent acquisition is a low rectangular container, 6in/15cm high, 21in/52cm long and 14in/35cm wide. It is glazed a deep, rich red, the colour of Turkish carpets, and I am planting it with sempervivums. These are not plants to set the world on fire, but they are intensely pleasing, symmetrical and perfectly made.

Ideally the pot should sit up on a shelf or table. I have not arranged this yet, but it is the kind of support that could easily be built into the side of a patio to give interest to a plain wall. The next pot I have my eye on is also Chinese, but glazed in brilliant turquoise, the colour of Egyptian faience. Clipped phillyrea would be just the thing to go with it. When I am tired of being sober I can fill it instead with a succession of wild 'Gudoshnik' tulips, orange feathered with cream and peach and red. The point of a patio is not merely to have it but to use it.

JOBS FOR THE MONTH

General

⚜ If you have a new lawn in mind, do not skimp on the preparation. Choose a seed mixture to suit the site. Shady lawns will need a higher percentage of coarse rye grass. Sheep's fescue will grow well in dry places.

⚜ This is an ideal month to plant bamboos. They make good screens but will not thrive in very exposed situations. They like good, moist soil. *Arundinaria nitida* is the most shade-tolerant, with purple-flushed canes and narrow bright green leaves.

⚜ Mulch trees and shrubs while the ground is still damp.

⚜ Freshly planted evergreens may need a temporary screen around them to prevent the foliage drying out.

Flowers

⚜ Thin out flowering shoots of mophead and lacecap hydrangeas, cutting a few of the old stems to ground level.

⚜ Sow petunias in a temperature of around 60°F/15°C.

⚜ Start thinking about stakes *before* your plants need them.

⚜ Prune hardy fuchsias, such as *F. magellanica*, down to ground level.

⚜ Cut back perovskia and romneya near the base of the stems.

⚜ If you have time to spare, deadhead daffodils to stop them wasting energy on seed production.

⚜ Lift and split hardy chrysanthemums that have overwintered outside.

⚜ Plant out sweet pea seedlings, providing support for the plants in the form of either bamboo canes or pea sticks.

⚜ Prune forsythia, cutting out some of the old wood each year. Aim for a three-year cycle, so that within that time, you have worked over the whole bush.

⚜ Towards the end of the month, start to harden off annuals ready for planting out in May.

⚜ Continue to sow hardy annuals outside where you want them to flower.

⚜ Protect the new spears of hosta foliage against slugs.

⚜ As hellebore flowers fade, new foliage starts pushing through from the base. Feed with a fertilizer high in potash at fortnightly intervals until mid-June (not later, or growth will be too soft).

⚜ Camellias may need picking over as they are reluctant to shed their flowers.

⚜ Various forms of primroses and polyanthus can be split and replanted now in ground refreshed with bonemeal and compost.

❧ If necessary, prune grey-leaved shrubs such as artemisia, phlomis, senecio, sage, santolina and rue, cutting out any growth damaged by wind or frost.

❧ Summer-flowering heathers – types of calluna, daboecia and erica – can also be sheared over now, as new shoots are beginning to grow.

❧ Christmas amaryllis die down messily about this time of year. When the foliage has withered naturally, lay the pot and its bulb on its side to rest in an airy, dry place. Next December, repot the bulb and start it into growth again.

❧ Begonias can be planted in pots and hanging baskets inside before being set out in May.

Vegetables

❧ Plant well-sprouted early potatoes, setting them about 6in/15cm deep and twice that distance apart.

❧ Try an early sowing of lettuce and endive.

❧ Plant onion sets about 4in/10cm apart in rows 12in/30cm apart.

❧ Sow radish, mustard and cress and more lettuce.

❧ Sow kohlrabi in shallow drills, thinning the seedlings later to give room for each plant to develop. They should be ready by July.

❧ For an early crop of French beans, sow seed indoors.

❧ Watch emerging pea crops carefully. They will be prone to attack from pigeons, rabbits, slugs and weasels.

Fruit

❧ Hoe carefully around raspberry canes to shift annual weeds. Do not delve too deep: raspberries are shallow-rooted.

❧ Remove and burn the greasebands put round fruit trees last autumn.

❧ Spread clean straw round strawberries and remove runners so that the plants concentrate on producing fruit.

Propagating

❧ Divide achillea, agapanthus, artemisia, arundinaria, carex, diascia, festuca, geranium, gunnera, heuchera, kniphofia, matteuccia, miscanthus, origanum, polygonum, sedum, sempervivum, stachys, tellima, tiarella.

❧ Take tip cuttings of abelia, acer, caryopteris, fuchsia, helichrysum, lavender.

❧ Set heather cuttings into individual small pots, using an ericaceous compost.

❧ Start to harden off cuttings of semi-tender shrubs in a cold frame if possible.

❧ Prick out seedlings of annuals as they develop their first true leaves, but keep them under cover.

M<u>AY</u>

An Englishman's Home is by his Lawn

Lawns would be all right were it not for lawnmowers. Each spring brings a fresh mowing drama. As the grass begins to grow and the first hints are dropped about the desirability of a close-mown sward to set off the daffodils, the children exchange meaningful glances round the kitchen table. There is a short period in their mid to late teens when children are strong enough, malleable enough and skint enough to mow on an agreeably regular basis. If only the mower were as tractable.

Starting it is the chief problem. The area to be mown is too big for an electric machine, which would get over this problem. The petrol-powered rotary engine has to be whirled into life like an outboard motor, with a cord wound round the flywheel.

Desperate tension mounts during the bursts of *musique concrète* that the machine goes in for while it decides whether it wants to cooperate. Usually it doesn't and another Saturday morning vanishes in the 25-mile trip to the millionaire mechanic at Medland, Sanders and Twose's agricultural depot.

Lawns are a particularly British fetish. There are sixteen million of them being fussed and fretted over, fed, sprinkled, spiked, raked and rolled. If you do everything that you are supposed to do to a lawn in a year, it can become the most demanding area of the garden. Also the most expensive.

I do not have high expectations of a lawn. It has only to be greenish and flattish. Daisies and the blue-flowered speedwell seem a positive benefit. This year a swarm of white violets have moved into the grass, which is even better. Weeds with wide spreading skirts – dandelions, plantains, thistles of any kind – are a menace, but it is quicker and far more satisfying to whip these out with a penknife than to spend hours like a donkey on a treadmill, spreading weed-killer over the whole sward.

This creed will be anathema to the fanatical aco-lytes for whom a single daisy can be cause for hara-kiri. These are more likely to be men than women. Perhaps it is the ritual that attracts: the twice-weekly cut, the edge clipping, the stripes. The need for stripes is particularly intriguing, but deeply ingrained enough for Flymo to have brought out the Hover-stripes, hover mowers that stripe as they cut as they hover. Previously only cylinder mowers and some types of rotary mower gave that desired effect.

The conviction that a garden is not a garden without a lawn results in swards bobbing up in some extraordinarily unsuitable places. In desert countries, they are the epitome of conspicuous consumption. Expatriate British marooned in Portugal, India and the Caribbean hang grimly on to their lawns, life rafts in a sea of strangeness.

MAY

You see them growing against all the odds in countries where they need watering for at least six hours a day to keep them alive. Conversely, in tropical countries, where magnificent aroids and bromeliads can give you all the ground cover you need, it seems contrary to insist on sheets of the broad-leaved weed they call grass, which in that hothouse climate grows so fast it needs cutting at least four times a week.

Perhaps there is some deep seated notion of security, of standards at work here. As long as we hang on to our lawns, we know where we stand. This was the territory mined so profitably by the early pioneers of the underground railways. Golders Green, Hendon and Finchley, a place of delightful prospects, sang the posters against sunlit images of semi-detached villas, each with its picket fence, its standard roses and its neatly edged patch of lawn.

Small town gardens are not the easiest places to grow lawns, especially where they are overhung by trees, but garden designers have an uphill struggle persuading garden owners that they will be as happy instead with paving, or pebbles or a thick bark mulch. Green is what the heart desires.

There are sound environmental reasons for choosing green, as turf merchants are quick to point out. Lawns absorb pollutants such as soot, dust and carbon dioxide. In the heat of summer, grass is considerably cooler than bare soil, very much cooler (up to 30°F/

16°C) than concrete paving. A lawn of roughly 290 square yards or metres is enough to keep a family of four in all the oxygen they can gulp. A study by the Lawn Institute in the US indicates that a well-kept lawn absorbs rainfall six times more effectively than a field of wheat. Where there are only hard surfaces in a garden, rainwater cannot be absorbed and re-used. It disappears into the drains.

Against the benefits, you must set some environmental disadvantages. The best-kept lawns are likely to be those with the least diversity of plants. The ideal is a monoculture: several million blades of fine grass living in a botanical ghetto, untroubled by interlopers such as daisy and celandine. Species richness is a key issue in the environment war. A regularly weed-killed lawn ends up in enemy lines.

And then there are lawnmowers. As yet, there is no legal requirement to fit catalytic converters to lawnmower engines, though in smog-ridden California there is increasing pressure by clean-air groups to control pollution caused by garden machinery.

The state's powerful Air Resources Board has the power to force manufacturers to act, even though changes would add another 25 per cent to the price of lawnmowers. The problem lies in the relative inefficiency of the two-stroke engine, which, the board has been told, for each horsepower produced, creates fifty times more pollution than a long-distance lorry.

In California, it is estimated that five per cent of all hydrocarbons and four per cent of the carbon monoxide in the atmosphere is produced by petrol-driven garden machinery. And there is the added problem of noise as sixteen million little juggernauts spring into action (or in our case, not) every weekend.

All in all, electric mowers are probably the cheapest and the least trouble, if you have the necessary cable and power point. Apart, that is, from the human-powered kind, but you have to be a more than usually good citizen, or have a patch only just large enough for a gnome to sit on, to push a hand mower about. According to research, five per cent of British lawn owners do still mow by hand; 84 per cent use electric mowers, the rest petrol.

Cutting widths vary: obviously the wider the machine, the less walking you have to do and the quicker the job gets done. How much quicker is one of those questions that turned the brain to jelly in school maths exams, but *Gardening from Which?* came up with the answer. To mow an average lawn with a 12in/300mm mower, you will walk just over half a mile/0.84km. If you use a 17in/420mm mower, you walk only three-quarters that distance, and the time spent mowing drops from 22 minutes to 16 minutes. Unfortunately, the magazine has no equally precise answer to the problem of recalcitrant starting motors.

WINDOWBOXES

Pubs are the places to see brilliant windowboxes and
hanging baskets. Is it beer dregs that makes the plants
flourish so? Or all the hot air produced by saloon bar
regulars? Lobelia is the common ingredient in most
of the plantings: dark-leaved, dark-flowered lobelia
with white petunias, pale blue lobelia with deep red
pelargoniums and silver fern. Hackneyed, you might
sneer, but these combinations are difficult to beat.

For summer windowboxes, you need flowers that
have the same unflagging determination to perform
as the young Shirley Temple. Pelargoniums, often
coaxed into bloom before they go on sale at garden
centres, are supreme in this respect. Their variety
means that you can easily furnish windowboxes with
nothing else: trailing ivy-leaved ones for the front,
multi-bloom varieties such as 'Sensation' for the bulk
of the planting with a few variegated types inter-
spersed for contrast.

To flower most abundantly pelargoniums need sun,
but a windowbox in full sun is more difficult to manage than one in part shade. Compost dries out faster;
watering may need to be done twice a day.

A windowbox looks best if it fits as exactly as possible the size of the window. Small plastic containers
balanced on large sills have an uneasy, we're-not-
stopping feel to them. Made-to-measure wooden

containers are ideal. You can line them with heavy-duty black polythene, a few holes punched in the bottom. The bigger the container and the larger the volume of compost, the easier it will be to keep.

Painting wooden boxes can trap you in a tyranny of annual repainting. Woodstains are less demanding and, watered down, give you some pleasantly murky greens and blues. Let the plants boss the box rather than the other way around.

Profusion is the effect that you want, but in a windowbox you won't get it without a dedicated regime of feeding and watering. Slow-release fertilizers are excellent for this kind of gardening. So are the expanded polystyrene granules you can buy which sop up water faster than sponges and then release it slowly as the plants need it. Both these can be mixed into the compost at planting time.

Plastic boxes are cheap, but are not always sufficiently sturdily made to take a full load of compost. They start buckling in the middle and sag outwards in a dispirited way. Whatever you use, make sure it is securely anchored. Some town houses still have the ornamental cast-iron surrounds of the late eighteenth and early nineteenth centuries to fence in windowboxes.

Often boxes look better from the outside than they do from indoors. Flowers naturally turn towards the light, so from inside you are backstage, as it were, looking at the supports rather than the painted back-drop. You can get over this by lowering the level of the windowbox slightly, so that you look down on your flowers, but whether this is possible depends on the type of windows and sills that you have.

For a suitably lush effect (and windowboxes must be lush – nothing looks meaner than a mean windowbox, its plants as distant as oases in the desert) you need plenty of leaf. Include at least one good foliage plant in each mixture. *Helichrysum petiolare* is a natural, because it is not too bossy, threads itself about well, climbs and cascades. The standard version has grey, felted leaves, but there is a good lime-coloured variety, 'Limelight', and a cream variegated one as well. The grey-leaved one loves heat and will not flag in a sun-baked position. The sulphurous one is better in part shade. Use them with marguerites (*Argyranthemum frutescens*), white petunias and shrubby santolina, with perhaps some variegated ginger mint binding the whole cast together.

An average sized windowbox, 30–32in/75–80cm long, will easily accommodate a dozen plants, perhaps four each of the marguerites and petunias, one helichrysum, one santolina and two ginger mints. This will give a cool effect – lost, though, if you live in a white-painted house. White-flowered windowboxes look best set against grubby stone, especially the dark grits and granites of the north.

MAY

Grey helichrysum also looks good weaving its way round ivy-leaved pelargoniums, such as pale pink 'Madame Crousse', with a mixture of lobelias stuffed into the gaps. *Lobelia* 'Cascade Mixture' trails elegantly and has flowers in a wide range of colours. Add some deep purple heliotrope if you want an extra benefit from your windowbox: it smells gorgeous.

For a much warmer effect, use the greeny-yellow helichrysum 'Limelight' with a golden variegated ivy and some brilliant yellow and blue pansies. These need regular dead-heading if you want them to give a long display, but they are reliable flowerers and have the sort of squidged-up faces that always make you smile. Ivy is very slow-growing, so you will need to splash out on some decent-sized plants. They are at least perennial and, with care, could be with you for several seasons. If you get tired of them in a windowbox, you can pot them up and use them as pot plants inside.

Nasturtiums are also plants that raise the spirits. There is nothing restrained about a nasturtium. It is a helter-skelter opportunist and will probably swamp any plants that you put with it. Use it on its own, sowing seeds direct into the windowbox. If it is too soon to get rid of your spring display, raise nasturtium plants in pots inside, planting them out at the end of May. 'Alaska' is a good mixture, with leaves splashed and mottled with cream.

Any annual that lolls gracefully is a natural con-
tender for a windowbox. The Swan River daisy
(*Brachycome iberidifolia*) could easily be used this way.
It has lax stems topped with purplish-blue daisy
flowers and the foliage is lush and ferny. The plants
do best if you pinch them back early in the season to
encourage thick, bulky growth. 'Purple Splendour'
from Thompson & Morgan is the only single colour,
but the mixture with blue, mauve and white flowers
is charming. The plants grow about 9in/23cm high,
do not immediately flag if they are dry at the roots
and flower for months. As they are quite delicate
they do not need anything too bossy with them. In
Garden Flowers from Seed Graham Rice suggests
threading a few black-eyed Susans (*Thunbergia alata*)
through them. The dwarf sweet pea 'Snoopea' might
also be a good companion.

❦

PLUGGING IN THE TULIP BULBS

I have been bombarded over the last couple of
months with circulars from the bank urging me to
borrow large sums of money to buy a new car or deck
out the kitchen or build an extension to the house.
None of these seemed worthwhile pursuits, so I wrote
to the manager suggesting that he instead lend me a
large sum of money to go on a bulb binge.

I am impatient to hurry on my life's work of growing every known variety of tulip before I die. He
replied with a po-faced letter saying that, while a set
of Formica tops or a kitchen cabinet were in order,
he did not consider expenditure on bulbs the kind
of activity in which the bank would wish to get
involved. The man is clearly mad.

The problem is that so sure was I that the bank
would enthusiastically endorse this endeavour, I had
already sent off my order with cheque. We will have
to cut down on rations elsewhere. Bean soup and
biscuits must be the order of the day. If the bank
manager had seen the border of 'Magier' tulips this
spring, I am sure he would have been won over.
Perhaps the thing to do would be to invite him over.
If that doesn't work, I shall have to change banks.

'Magier' was the great hit of last season's tulips. It
is a cottage tulip, or single late, as they are sometimes
called, flowering through the second half of May.
The petals are soft milky white splashed with purple
round the edges. As the flower ages, which it does
gracefully and well (a worthwhile attribute), the
whole thing darkens and purple leaches out from the
edges through the whole of the surface of the petals.

It is the most graceful, pleasing late tulip I have
ever grown; tall – more than 2ft/60cm – but sturdy.
None snapped. They more than made up for the
sad disappointment of the early crocus planted round

their feet in the same narrow border.

This was 'Ladykiller', a variety of C. *vernus* I had admired at the Royal Horticultural Society's show. The flowers were (when I saw them on the show bench) a dramatic combination of purple outside and white inside. In the garden few came up, which may have been the mice's fault rather than the bulbs', but those that did had weak stems that keeled over as soon as the flower began to develop.

Much more fun were the fat Dutch crocus 'Remembrance' which burst from the ground with touching enthusiasm and taught me once again the important lesson that you can be too refined in gardening.

There was one disaster among the tulips too, a double early called 'Peach Blossom'. I had warmed to the double early after the spectacular success of 'Alice Leclercq', orange-red with a yellow edge. This is no longer available from Parkers, where I originally got it, nor from any other catalogues I have to hand, though all offer 'Peach Blossom'. This turned out not to be peachy at all, but a hideous and strident pink, with a formless flower. 'Squat and messy,' I have written in my tulip book. Unfortunately 'Alice Leclercq' did not prove to be a stayer, but I bet 'Peach Blossom' is and that next spring it will be there again in the front border, goading me for my foolishness in ever believing a catalogue description.

I am not giving up on the double earlies. Next

season I am going to try 'Monte Carlo', lemon-yellow outside, deep golden-yellow inside, slightly taller than 'Peach Blossom' at 16in/40cm and flowering slightly later towards the end of April.

Although I have not tried it myself, I saw some good bowls of double early tulips forced like hyacinths in a friend's house this spring. Used in this way, you could have 'Monte Carlo' in bloom by mid-February. To do this you need to plant earlier than you would outside.

Cover the bulbs with soil in a container and set them outside in a cool, shaded corner where you can cover the pot with a further 6in/15cm of earth. Leave them there until mid-January (with the earliest type) then bring them into a dark place indoors where the temperature does not get above 60°F/15°C. After two or three weeks, when the growth has been forced on, bring the bulbs into light and warmth for the flowers to develop. Either single or double earlies will respond well to this treatment, though some, such as 'Princess Irene', marigold-orange feathered with violet, need to be left outside until mid-February.

I had never grown the famous tulip 'Madame Lefeber' until this season and tried it in the same tub where I had previously grown the outstanding and similarly coloured 'Cantate'. Both are the same type of tulip, from the Fosteriana group, but I thought though 'Madame Lefeber' was good, 'Cantate' was better, for it had much better foliage, silkily shining.

'Madame Lefeber' was a couple of weeks earlier in bloom, with long thin buds and greyish leaves. Next season I will try a different red tulip to go with the lime-green sulphurous bracts of the big euphorbia, E. *characias*. The Fosteriana type 'Princeps' is the one I have gone for, vermilion scarlet 12in/30cm high.

It is perhaps contrary to assess tulips by foliage – leaves are not one of the family's great strengths – but this is an even better reason to commend those that produce more than a few tatty furls. 'Berlioz' has good leaves, like many of the Kaufmanniana types, and did well in pots by my back door. It has slightly pointed petals of good clear lemonish-yellow with a red base. The leaves are well mottled and streaked with purplish-brown on a grey-green base. It was very short, only 5in/13cm or so, but well-balanced, unlike the monstrous 'Peach Blossom'.

A miniature narcissus, 'Minnow', did well on the bank, flowering in March with pale lemon flowers on 7in/18cm stems. Miniatures are not my forte, but I am developing an area where the Lilliputians can grow together undwarfed by the oversized mob that rules the rest of the garden.

Species tulips I thought would make a good follow-on for 'Minnow'. The two that have been doing their bit are *T. saxatilis*, which grows wild in Crete and Turkey, and *T. urumiensis* from north-east Iran.

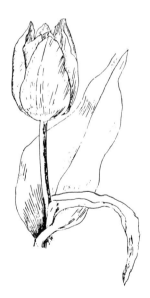

T. saxatilis has glossy leaves and bright pinkish-lilac flowers in May, well-timed to succeed 'Minnow'. *T. urumiensis* is even smaller, about 4in/10cm high, with golden yellow flowers, each petal washed over with bronze on the reverse.

My particular weakness is for tulips that are streaked and feathered in contrasting colours like 'Magier'. I used to buy Rembrandts by the score, until suppliers stopped offering them. The markings that distinguish the Rembrandts are caused by a virus, which can affect other tulips that are not supposed to be streaked or mottled. This made them unpopular.

The closest you can get now is a pseudo-Rembrandt mixture such as that offered by de Jager. 'Unsurpassed for artistic effect,' they say, a mixture made up themselves from 'flamed varieties in distinct colours'. These are Rembrandts by design rather than by disease. None of the ones that came up had the deep, rich, tawny colours of the tulips that still bob up from my original plantings. Most are a combination of cream, feathered with purple. Some have weird fasciated stems, two tulips welded into one, bearing two flowers at the top.

If you ever see a tulip called 'Absalom', buy it immediately. It has exactly the quality of the old Rembrandts in rich chocolate. The catch is that you hardly ever do see it. I would gladly bankrupt myself for a patch of this.

More Haste – Less Taste

No new gardener takes over a garden without having some ideas about the plants that he would like to see in it. Even those whose knowledge does not extend beyond recognizing a daffodil when they see it will bring to their new plots a Proustian jumble of *plantes perdues*: the smell of an American currant that made a base camp in childhood, the silhouette of a magnolia that they passed on the way to school.

The fat double daisies that grew in my grandmother's walled garden are one of my talismans. We reached her garden by crossing the river Usk in a small flat-bottomed punt, wound over by the ferryman who lived in a hut on the far side. The daisies lined all the paths in the garden and were the only flowers I was allowed to pick. Now they line mine.

Although I doubt the value of a pencil and paper in designing the basic layout of a garden, for sorting out plants they are essential. First, put on the paper everything that you have a vague desire to grow. If there really is nothing lurking in the back of your mind, visit a large and well-stocked garden centre. Write down the name of anything you like the look of. Do not buy anything yet. This is the hardest part, but, for the plants' sake, vital.

Buy instead, or borrow, a good illustrated reference

book, such as the Reader's Digest *Encyclopaedia of Garden Plants* or the RHS *Gardeners' Encyclopaedia of Plants and Flowers* and use it to add to your list and to look up plants already on it.

This may lead to some thinning out. You may have written rhododendron in large letters at the top of your wanted page, but will learn, as you riffle through your reference book, that rhododendrons can only be expected to flourish in acid soil. If this is not what you have got (and by this stage you should know things of that nature), then strike out rhododendron or make a note to grow it in a tub filled with special ericaceous compost. The chief lime-haters are the plants of the classic woodland gardens: rhododendrons, azaleas, camellias, pieris.

Some plants, like people, have decided preferences as to where they most want to put down roots, the horticultural equivalent of Tooting, Widnes or Rye. If you have admired the blue of a ceanothus in the garden centre and have thought that it would look very nice spreadeagled against the north wall of your house, think again. Ceanothus feel about north walls what we feel about Siberia. They are Californians by birth and a south or a west wall is the least you can do to make them feel at home.

Somewhere, of course, most probably in the south-west some clever clogs will have a ceanothus flourishing on a north wall and he may well be a beginner. The exception is what makes gardening interesting, but novices should not bank on exceptions.

This thinning out should leave you with a list of plants that have a decent chance of flourishing in your soil and in the situations that you have planned for them. The next task is to scribble beside each plant an approximate time of flowering. You may find that this leaves you with an explosion of happenings in May and very little for the rest of the year.

If this is just what you want – fine. If not, snoop around other people's gardens, return to the well-thumbed reference book and start on the list again. The RHS encyclopaedia is arranged in a seasonal fashion, which makes filling the gaps a relatively easy process. For those in too much of a hurry to do either, here is a starter pack of plants for walls and fences.

North

Hydrangea petiolaris is a climbing member of the hydrangea family with large lacecap heads of cream-white flowers in June. Once established, it sticks itself on to a wall in the same way as ivy. The leaves are a brilliant fresh green when they first come out and, in some autumns, change to a good clear yellow. Do not count on the autumn act, however. The plant sometimes seems slow to get going. This is often because it does not want to risk too much growth until it feels securely attached to something. Pin growths tightly to their support and if the thing still will not cling, strain it upwards with some twine. Mulch it each spring with well-decayed muck or compost. No regular pruning is necessary, but you can snip off the dead flower heads in March before new growth begins again.

Jasminum nudiflorum is common, but for a good reason. Little else chooses to start flowering in November and at that nadir of the year, the bright yellow flowers are particularly welcome. It is a lax, droopy thing, totally unable to hold itself up without support so you will need to pin it up against whatever you want it to decorate. If you are short of space, grow it in tandem with the hydrangea, which will be bare by the time the jasmine's display starts. The jasmine itself is too spindly to get in the hydrangea's way during summer.

East

Pyracantha has neat evergreen leaves which are just as useful as its much vaunted berries. Some evergreens are essential in a well furnished garden. All have white, hawthorn-like flowers in June, but the berries can be yellow, orange or red, depending on variety. 'Mohave' is a good, disease-resistant variety with orange-red fruits. Pyracanthas look much more interesting if you train them. The growths are naturally long and straight and fall very easily into parallel lines, squares and diamonds. No regular pruning is necessary. Tie in the growths you want to keep and cut back the rest close to the main stem.

Clematis, a late-flowering variety, can be used with the pyracantha to tide it over the lull between flowers and berries. Clematis, which have no backbone at all, are much happier wandering through other plants than spreadeagled on their own on trellis. 'Comtesse de Bouchaud' or 'Huldine' will both be well set off against the pyracantha foliage.

West

Rose – there has to be a rose somewhere in this group – but which is impossible to say. My own preference is for the cluster-flowered, slightly wild-looking types such as 'Wedding Day'. This is a very vigorous rose that can reach 30ft/10m, with wide trusses of sweet-smelling small, single, white flowers with prominent orange stamens. It is not repeat-flowering, which may be held against it. 'Hamburger Phoenix' is technically a modern shrub rose rather than a climber, but it can easily reach 8ft/2.5m and is excellent on a wall, with loose clusters of large semi-double crimson flowers, followed by good hips. Cut out some old wood of each in early spring and tie in new growth as it arises. *Chaenomeles* (japonica or flowering quince) is an easy-going spring-flowering shrub straight out of a

119

Japanese painting. In a mild winter the flowers, in shades of scarlet, orange, pink and white, may start as early as January and continue through until April. 'Knap Hill Scarlet' has large brilliant red flowers, 'Rowallane' is a bloody crimson colour, 'Nivalis' pure white. It will thrive in any soil, especially if you mulch it well with compost in spring. Keep it trained flat against the wall for the best effect. Cut off any shoots that you cannot tie in after flowering in May.

South

Ceanothus have the best blue flowers of any shrub. Deciduous late-flowering varieties are said to be hardier than the evergreen early ones. Despite this, I suggest C. *impressus*, only half-hardy but covered in April and May with clusters of small, deep blue flowers. C. *thyrsiflorus* is said to be one of the hardiest of the evergreens and flowers in May and June with pale blue flowers. Mulch well each spring. No regular pruning is necessary, but growths should be tied in close against the wall.

Cytisus battandieri (Moroccan broom) is the final ingredient, with stubby hanging bunches of bright yellow flowers which smell of pineapple. Its leaves are as good as the flowers: clover-shaped and covered with soft, silvery hairs. It will grow up to 18ft/5.4m against a support: tie in lax stems regularly. It needs no feeding or pruning, but plenty of sun.

JOBS FOR THE MONTH

General

❧ Be patient with any shrubs you think may have been killed over winter. They may yet show signs of life.

❧ This is a good time to attack ground elder with a weedkiller based on glyphosate. It is said to be most susceptible just as the leaves have unfurled. More than one application may be needed.

❧ Mulching will keep down the population of easy annual weeds such as meadowgrass and groundsel.

❧ If May is warm, greenfly multiply fast. If the ladybirds are not keeping up, spray with a specific insecticide.

Flowers

❧ Tie in new growths of rambling roses, so that they do not lash about.

❧ Sow perennials for flowering next year. *Aquilegia alpina* is a fairly dwarf columbine with flowers of a particularly good blue. Sow seed about ¼in/5mm deep in a seed bed outside. Plant out in late summer for flowers next spring.

❧ Continue to clear wallflowers and tulips from tubs and beds to make room for the next plantings.

❧ Thin out seedlings of hardy annuals that you have sown direct outside.

❧ Continue to sow annuals such as Shirley poppy, love-in-a-mist, night-scented stock, clarkia and cornflower outside where they are to flower.

❧ Replant windowboxes and hanging baskets with plants for summer. It should now be safe to put fuchsias and pelargoniums outside in containers.

❧ Prune wall-trained chaenomeles after it has finished flowering, cutting back each of the previous season's growths to within two or three buds. Tie in new growths of solanum.

❧ Plant out young plants of *Eccremocarpus scaber* at the foot of a sunny wall and give them something to scramble up.

❧ Trim hedges of *Berberis darwinii* as soon as the flowers are over.

❧ Sow biennials (such as Canterbury bell, verbascum and wallflower) and perennials (such as aquilegia, lupin, oriental poppy and delphinium) in drills outside.

❧ Seed of viola, pansies and different forms of primrose and polyanthus can also be sown outside now for transplanting later. Choose a shady spot for these.

❧ Nip out weak growths in congested clumps of delphiniums.

❧ Sift fresh soil or compost over clumps of saxifrage to fill in any dead patches.

❦ Continue to deadhead daffodils, but do not cut away foliage, however untidy, until it dies down naturally.

❦ Lilies will benefit from a mulch of leaf-mould or compost to keep the roots cool. Those in pots will need a weekly feed.

Vegetables

❦ Set celery plants in trenches, in the bottom of which you should have put plenty of muck, covered by soil. Plants should be about 12in/30cm apart in staggered double rows about 9in/23cm apart down the sides of the trench.

❦ Sow sweetcorn in a warm sheltered spot outside. Plant the seeds in a square block in a grid pattern about 18in/45cm apart each way. This helps with pollination.

❦ Start to earth up early potatoes. Finish planting maincrop potatoes.

❦ Make further sowings of lettuce, radish, cress.

❦ Sow maincrop peas and set up pea sticks, netting or some other support for well advanced early peas.

❦ Set out plants of broccoli and curly kale.

❦ Watch out for blackfly homing in on broad beans and pinch out the tips of the plants if they settle.

❦ Outdoor cucumbers and courgettes can be started off in small pots inside at the beginning of the month. Sow seeds two to a pot and cover with plastic film and paper until the seedlings emerge. Pluck out the weaker of the two seedlings, if both have germinated.

❦ Seed of outdoor tomatoes such as 'Red Alert' and 'Tornado' can also be started off inside at the beginning of the month.

Fruit

❦ Thin out raspberry canes, if suckers are growing very thickly.

❦ Thin the fruit on outdoor peaches and apricots, leaving roughly one fruit for each foot of branch.

❦ Cordon fruit trees, like espaliers and fans, have a habit of throwing out shoots where you do not want them. Pinch out any that are pointing directly into the wall or that are too close together.

Propagating

❦ Make layers of cornus, corylopsis, cotinus, ivy, magnolia, parthenocissus.

❦ Take tip cuttings of abutilon, ceratostigma, cotinus, fuchsia, lilac.

❦ Gradually harden off trays of bedding plants before setting them out.

❦ Plant out well-rooted cuttings of silver-leaved and semi-tender shrubs to grow on in a nursery plot.

JUNE

FURRY BUT NO FRIENDS OF MINE

There has been another saga with the sheep. Starved of food in their own scruffy paddock, they leaned on the fence that separates us from them and barged, in their hideously destructive way, through the flowers on the bank towards an oasis of green in the vegetable patch. Only some magnificent tackles by our middle daughter, a rugby groupie, saved the day. The sheep were forcibly ejected and a guard mounted on the mangled fence until the farmer could come to fix it.

All this, combined with an avalanche of PR handouts exhorting us to be kind to our 'furry friends' as they are still astonishingly described, made me feel that the gardener is getting a raw deal. Animals are becoming positively uppity. Of course, sheep are an optional (and undesirable) extra, but my garden is heaving with wildlife. Animals need no further encouragement.

Over the last couple of months they have been extraordinarily bold and insolent. I have always known that they were lurking about, like guerrilla fighters, ready to leap in and wreak havoc when my back was turned, but now they are so sure of their supremacy that they saunter about munching, tunnelling, reproducing in full sight.

I went up the bank a little while ago to do some weeding. A fox cub, about the size of a cat, came lazily out from the undergrowth, sat on a prized patch of *Aster lateriflorus* and watched me in a bored fashion. It unnerved me. It was so obviously hanging about, waiting for me to get out of the way so it could get on with its business. I gave in and left the weeding.

After that first occasion, fox cubs sprouted all over the place, underneath the philadelphus I thought I would prune, behind the rubus that needed sorting out. All of them had that easy confidence, bordering on arrogance, that is supposed to come only from years of expensive education. All managed to dissuade me from doing what I had set out to do in what I thought was my own garden.

Even the moles, which generally keep themselves to themselves, have been acting out of character. I was standing on the path the other day doing a ruminative bit of dead-heading when a mole ran over my feet. In an acre and a half of garden, I thought this was a bit thick. I hate to feel crowded. It had plenty of other places in which to practise the 100-metre dash. Doggedly territorial, however, it ran back again, taking the same, you would have thought pig-headed, line over the insteps, through the laces and down the side of the sole, disappearing at last into the verbascums. I couldn't take any more and picking up my feet like a trained trotter, returned to the house, beaten again.

Another mole – or perhaps the same malevolent mole, who knows? – made a vicious attack on a new path that had taken us more than three years to complete. It is laid with paving stones surrounded by an intricate pattern of round cobbles. The path was alongside a bed full of good, rich friable earth, but the mole chose instead to tunnel his way along the path heaving half Chesil beach on his back in the process. The route he took is still obvious to us. Although re-set, the disturbed stones have a tipsy air about them, as if at odds with the planned regularity of the rest of the cobbles.

A mole also subverted my plans to plant a new hebe dropped off by a passing friend. I had been wandering around for some time in the evening, plant in one hand, trowel in the other, wondering where to put it. (Planned mass plantings are not my forte. I like the random arrival of plants and the consequent opportunities this presents to shamble about, weighing up possible homes.)

Finally, I fixed on a spot, close to some primulas which would furnish the ground in late spring before the hebe had much to show, and reasonably sheltered from the north wind that wiped out most of my other hebes in the last bad winter. As I was gazing at the spot rolling the thoughts round in my head, discarding the notion of a white phlox with the hebe, wondering whether I should fetch the bonemeal, the ground began to heave and shake. A molehill rose up on the very spot I had chosen for the hebe. The mole himself soon bobbed out from the top of the heap like a gunner coming up from a gun emplacement. By now, perhaps over-sensitive to threats of invasion, I thought I detected a scheming, predatory expression on the mole's face as we gazed at each other over a yard of no-man's-land. He showed no sign of shifting his ground. Wimpish in the extreme, I tried to pretend that I had another perfectly good place for the hebe.

In part this increasing boldness must result from the death of my dog, nineteen years old and now buried in the garden. She spent a good deal of her time poking about the place, ambling round the paths, sniffing in holes, acting as a greater deterrent than I realized. She never caught anything, but, like a policeman on the beat, symbolized a kind of law and order that has now completely broken down.

Always mindful of where her next tin of Pedigree Chum was coming from, she obviously felt that, all things considered, it was as well to throw in her lot with me rather than with the army of insurgents lurking outdoors.

Her occasional transgressions generally took place outside the boundaries of the garden. Once, round about one o'clock on a Sunday, she came purposefully through the gate with a roast chicken in her mouth.

With a ghastly inevitability she was followed a quarter of an hour later by three campers who had been having a pre-lunch drink in the pub. Their chicken, they supposed, was cooling off in their tent. As it happened, I too was cooking a roast chicken that day. They had ours and we in our turn went to the pub to recoup our losses.

Rabbits are the worst of the furry mob. It was perfectly respectable to look on rabbits as nuisances until Richard Adams came along and in *Watership Down* imbued the pests with saintly mysticism and heroic grandeur. Heroic and mystical though they may be, they still eat what they shouldn't and tunnel like sappers where I wish they wouldn't.

One orderly tunnel, purposefully made, I could accept. The maddening thing is that they keep changing their minds about where they want to go. You would think that after all these millennia of tunnelling they could tell a decent site from a bummer. Instead, they launch enthusiastically into a bed, sending buried tulip bulbs, young primulas and wallflowers flying in all directions, and then lose interest. If they completely lost interest it would not matter. But, after an absent-minded spell, taste-testing various violas and pinks, they start equally furious operations in a different patch of ground.

All in all, what with these and the hordes of lay-about birds that lounge around the soft fruit patch languidly observing my futile attempts to scrabble together enough redcurrants for a summer pudding (and, heaven knows, from five bushes I should have enough), I am off wildlife.

A vole came in from the courtyard and sat watching television with the children this week. He seemed friendly, they reported, but it may be a feint. Having taken over the garden, the animals perhaps now have designs on the house. My next report may come to you from an underground bunker.

❦

PTERRIBLE NAMES

'What's in a name?' asked Shakespeare's Juliet. If you are called *Polystichum angulare divisilobum plumosum densum erectum*, the answer is 'Too much.' Names are the fern family's biggest problem. It is not their fault, of course. Point the accusing finger at Victorian collectors.

The fern craze was at its height in the middle of the nineteenth century. *The Fern Garden* written by Shirley Hibberd, the mass communicator, the Geoff Hamilton of his day, was published in 1869 and went through eight editions in as many years.

Great collections were made – at the expense of native habitats – and the British Pteridological Society set up shop. Obfuscation is not a prime requirement for members, although it may seem so. Pteridological is a pterrible mouthful. Fern Society would have been a friendlier option.

The Society was formed in Cumbria, where on 23 September 1891 at Mr Wiper's Rooms, Strickland Gate, Kendal, the first members gathered together. Borrowdale and the limestone pavements nearby were favourite hunting grounds for Victorian fern fanciers.

Ferns fuel a collector's avarice because, spontaneously, they do such silly things. Five of the British native species have an irresistible urge to try out new ideas. They grow tassels like bunches of parsley at the end of their fronds. They subdivide wildly to make patterns as complex as the Delta of the Nile. A perfectly sensible fern like the hart's tongue, with a plain green strap-shaped leaf, will suddenly take it into its head to perm its edges into a series of frilly curves, or try out a black stem instead of a green one. As each permutation arose, the fern fanciers gave that plant a fresh tag, bolting an extra descriptive bit of botanical Latin on to the existing generic name, rather as the Germans build up their portmanteau words.

Even if you restricted yourself to collecting variants of hardy British native ferns, you could still find fifty different kinds for the garden, the largest group coming from the buckler ferns, types of *Dryopteris*.

Ferns tend to creep up on you slowly, after you have had a long fling with colour. Grace is their chief attribute. They do not leap up and down saying 'Look at me!'. They quietly get on with what they have been doing for the last four hundred million years, unconcerned by the fickle vagaries of fashion.

Hot thin chalky ground and wildly windswept terrain are the only places where you might have difficulty persuading ferns to grow. In town gardens they are ideal, particularly for the rather difficult narrow borders that often run down alongside the passage from back door to garden.

Hart's tongues (*Phyllitis scolopendrium*), together with a few of the lacier types of fern such as polypodys and lady ferns, would do well in this sort of position – often rather dark, but cool, which ferns like, and damp. Plant snowdrops with them, followed by scillas and autumn-flowering cyclamen. The border will look after itself and shine for the whole of the year.

Symmetry is built into every fern's soul. That is what gives them such grace. They are stayers, too. Although not technically evergreen, the hart's tongues give an evergreen effect, for the old, strappy leaves survive all through the winter until the new fronds begin to unfurl. Then – as with all ferns – you should cut away the old foliage so that you can enjoy the extraordinary drama of the new ferns unfolding. The shapes are New Age ballet.

JUNE

131

Some ferns are meatier than others. The common
polypody (*Polypodium vulgare*) is the sort of a fern a
child might draw: a midrib with leaflets sprouting
along it at regular intervals. It grows along the horizontal branches of an old espalier pear tree trained
over our courtyard door. In dry weather it crinkles
up to nothing, but at the first drop of rain it expands
again, like a Japanese paper flower dropped in water.

Its cousin, *P. vulgare* 'Cornubiense', comes from
Cornwall and is much more complicated. The frond
of the common polypody is never more than about
3in/75mm wide. 'Cornubiense' makes a much broader
frond, all its leaflets or pinnae subdividing into
further sections and overlaying each other quite
densely. It has the useful attribute of growing its new
fronds in late July and looking its best in August,
when other greenery is beginning to look tired.

The common polypodys like good drainage, as you
can tell from the places where they put themselves
in the garden. Stony soil is ideal and they will also
colonize the north faces of stone walls. Humus in the
soil, or added as a mulch in autumn or spring when
you are planting, encourages ferns to do their best.

The fashion in the nineteenth century was to col-
lect ferns together in special ferneries. 'To retire from
the full glare of noon and the flower garden with all
its brilliant colours and somewhat stiff and formal
trimness, into the cool retirement . . . in which

Ferns generally luxuriate makes a most refreshing change to both body and mind,' wrote David Thomson in his *Handy Book of the Flower Garden* published in 1868. He was head gardener to Lady Hamilton at Archerfield in East Lothian, which became a role model for Victorian gardens, as Sissinghurst is for many people today.

Thomson recommended that ferns, 'those denizens of shade and rock, should occupy some quiet and shady and, if possible, romantic retreat'. Romance is always in short supply, but the other two elements should be borne in mind when you are thinking of where to put ferns.

'Quiet' is an interesting word for Thomson to have used. Ferns *are* quiet. They couldn't cope with the razzmatazz of the herbaceous border. They are well set off against stone or rotting tree stumps, if you happen to have any of those about. Some of the tallest sorts, such as the male fern (*Dryopteris filix-mas*), which throws up an elegant sheaf of fronds, can be used alone or as promontory plants, to mark a turn in a path, or stand either side of a crossing point.

In mixed plantings, the lacy kinds, lady ferns and male ferns, look best when paired with plants that have solid, rounded leaves. Bergenia is a natural companion. So are hostas of various sorts, especially late-flowering *Hosta plantaginea*, with bright green glossy heart-shaped leaves and lily-scented white flowers.

JUNE

133

Epimediums also provide the right sort of companionship for ferns, fiddling around close to the ground while the ferns erupt in fountains over them. The shuttlecock fern (*Matteuccia struthiopteris*) looks particularly good grown like this.

Since ferns have a fiendishly complicated sex life, propagation is best left to the experts. Some ferns, such as the polypodys, run about at the root and you can separate pieces from the main stock without too much anguish. As for the rest – leave them in peace.

⁓❀⊛❀⁓

HERCULES OF THE VEGETABLE PLOT

You will not find serious vegetable growers poncing about with sweetcorn, aubergines, fennel or kohlrabi. Onions, leeks, potatoes, carrots, parsnips and cauliflower are the staples of the show bench. If you start winning prizes with this double trinity of vegetables then you might meet George Payne one day. He is a Dorset shepherd, or rather was, for he is supposed to be retired, but he is still much in demand for trimming out sheep for the show pen and a thousand and one other jobs that most other shepherds have forgotten how to do.

He started gardening seriously on retirement, and soon had a sideboard stuffed full of challenge cups, shields and mugs, with a silver bowl on the top that is almost big enough to bath a baby in.

His forcing ground – garden seems too mild a word for it – lies round a solidly built post-war council house in Maiden Newton, Dorset. Two immaculately dug plots of ground lie on either side of the path to the front door. At the back is a ramshackle collection of greenhouses, polythene shelters and enough oil drums to equip several Caribbean steel bands. 'I don't waste time on frills,' said Mr Payne unnecessarily.

The oil drums with the bottoms knocked out make carrot and parsnip pens. No self-respecting showman now dares turn up at a show with a carrot less than 2ft/60cm long. Parsnips can easily outstrip them. First the oil drums are filled with sand. Then Mr Payne bores five or six holes to the bottom of the drum. By wiggling the long iron crowbar about, he produces a hole 2–3in/50–75mm across. This is painstakingly filled with the finest compost that man's ingenuity can devise. On top of each of these bore-holes of unalloyed nutrition, he sows a couple of seeds – five barrels of carrots and five of parsnips in all.

After germination, he thins out the also-rans to leave one seedling on each core. Then it is a matter of watering and waiting, until he tackles the Herculean task of getting the monster vegetables out of the oil drums and on to the show bench.

He sowed his carrot seed in mid-April. Onions went in on Boxing Day, leeks in mid-December. The

JUNE

length of the growing season is all with these two vegetables.

Barter with a local builder got Mr Payne enough battens and polythene to run up a leek house and an onion house. Under polythene, the onions grow faster and ripen better. The seedlings, first sown in a seed tray, were then potted into 2½in/6cm pots. The best sixty were moved into 5in/12cm pots.

When, in mid-April, the best forty had five leaves showing, they were planted out in their special shelter. They are watered with rain water ('bloody rubbish' is all that Mr Payne has to say about the other stuff), like the leeks in their house across the way.

The leeks need extra cosmetic treatment. They are fitted with collars made from damp-course material wrapped round a broom handle to make neat cylinders. This blanches the stem of the leek and, as it grows, it gets fitted with even longer damp-course collars. Each leek is staked, so that the leaves are all held up together in a tidy sheath.

The patience needed for all this fiddling perhaps only comes with age, for you rarely see young exhibitors queuing up for their first prizes. Patience and, of course, time is what it takes. Mr Payne is usually in his greenhouses by six in the morning.

Attention to detail is also important. The Payne compost mix is seven parts loam, three of peat and one of grit. To this basic mixture, George Payne adds

Vitax Q4 fertilizer, some Seagold seaweed fertilizer and his own magic ingredient, made from crumbled cow pats which he collects from a neighbour's pasture and spreads out in his greenhouse. When they are tinder-dry, he bashes them up with a hammer till they are the consistency of tobacco. In this form, it is added to the compost. 'I fancy it puts a better colour in the leaves,' he says. 'I bring home sheep manure, too, soak it in a bucket and use the liquid as a feed. It makes good strong plants.' Peat he has little time for. It dries out too quickly in his opinion and lacks body.

Didn't he ever get tired of parsnips, leeks and onions, I inquired? Wasn't he ever tempted, say, by courgettes? 'Courgettes!' he said contemptuously. 'Where's the challenge in courgettes? I have had a go at cucumbers once or twice, but the buggers won't grow straight. I think they need a house on their own. They are difficult to work in with other things.' You could tell that cucumbers interested him, with their possibility of mammoth growth.

It is my belief that sometime soon, another home-made greenhouse is going to be squeezed on to that small plot at the back. From that greenhouse will emerge cucumbers whose magnificent physique will be immortalized in folk song and in a legend. If the supply of cow dung keeps up, I see nothing to stop George Payne.

JUNE

GRACE AND FLAVOUR IN THE HERB BED

I suspect that people who make herb gardens also like filing systems. There is an irresistible urge in a herb garden to classify, sort and arrange. All mints here. All sages there. All herbs mentioned in Gerard's *Herbal* in one corner. All herbs used for dyeing in another. The search for order may also be mixed with a fuzzy sort of nostalgia: herb-strewn floors, natural medicines.

Herb gardens are also popular since they can be fitted into the tiniest of spaces. Formality suits them, but any patterns that you draw up should not be too intricate. Herbs flop about a good deal and may not appreciate the fact that they are ruining the finer points of the symmetry you strove for over weeks. A simple chequerboard with alternate squares filled with gravel would save the need for making paths.

A different kind of framework can be made with box, but it will take a few years to grow into a decently bulky edging. A square planted round with box and then sub-divided with more box into a trellis of diamond shapes makes a strong design for plants.

In choosing herbs, you must decide how much you are going to cheat. A herb garden is at its peak for a month in midsummer. If you want your patch to work harder than that for its living, then you should think of planting tulips for an early display among the emerging herbs, and bringing in pots of scented-leaf pelar-goniums, nasturtiums or heliotrope to keep the show going in late summer.

You will also need to think about some plants to give height, unless you are specifically aiming at a low Persian carpet effect of thyme and marjoram, chervil, parsley and mints. Standard roses and honey-suckles associate well with herbs and give extra help-ings of colour and scent. I have a great weakness also for standard gooseberries, which have neither, but which make me laugh.

Angelica is a splendidly statuesque plant, usually treated as a biennial. Foliage is a bright, light green and in the second year the plant throws up huge rounded flower heads of pale yellow-green. The whole thing stands as tall as a man and it also takes up a lot of sideways space.

The stems for candying should be cut in early June before the plant gets too stringy. Chop them into short lengths and cook them in a little water until it has all evaporated. Cover the stems with sugar, using equal weights of sugar and stem, and leave for two days. Cook again until the stems look translucent, then drain off the liquid. Lay the stems out on a tray, sprinkle with more sugar and leave them in a cool oven until they have stiffened.

Fennel also gives sculptural height to a herb garden. There is a superb bronze-leaved variety called

JUNE

Foeniculum vulgare purpureum with filigree foliage topped by flat heads of golden flowers in July. It also grows tall but does not need so much lateral space as the angelica. Both these herbs will seed themselves about furiously. Be ruthless about pulling up and discarding the emerging seedlings.

In a most simplistic way, herbs can be split into two divisions: the Mediterranean aromatics such as thyme, rosemary and marjoram that need hot sun and poor soil to feel at home, and others such as mint, comfrey and borage that like a cooler, richer soil to grow in. If one side of your projected herb patch is sunnier than the other, save it for the Mediterranean sunbathers.

Thymes particularly resent being in damp, clogged soil and will quickly show their displeasure by rotting away. Fast-draining soil in full sun is what they need. Plant creeping forms, varieties of *Thymus serpyllum*, in cracks in the paths of herb gardens. Use the upright shrubby varieties in beds. Lemon thyme, *T. × citriodorus*, is particularly good for stuffings and herb bread. Cut down some of the shoots in June to encourage plenty more new leaf for the rest of the season. Take cuttings in June and July. Use side shoots about 2–3in/50–75mm long with a heel attached and line them out in sandy, friable soil.

Mints have a bad name for putting themselves where they are not wanted, but as the running roots are quite close to the surface, they are easy enough to dig up. The common mint is M. *spicata*, or spearmint, and is very easy to grow. My favourite is the brilliant yellow variegated variety, *Mentha × gentilis* 'Variegata'. Its common name is gingermint. It is lower-growing than the culinary variety, but has the same purplish flower spikes from July to September. Friends with exquisite palates insist that the round-leaved applemint, M. × *rotundifolia*, makes the best mint sauce.

Anyone who has taken up Indian cooking with Madhur Jaffrey may find themselves short of the coriander leaves she uses by the handful. Coriander is easily grown from seed, but some varieties leap very quickly into flower, with not much leaf. Suffolk Herbs offer a variety specially selected for its leafiness, although it also produces seed heads. Sow seed in April in an open, sunny situation. Plants grow up to about 2ft/60cm with heads of pinky-mauve flowers.

Dill has feathery leaves like fennel and also grows well from seed. You can eat it raw in salads or cooked with fish or vegetables, particularly potatoes and beans. The seeds can be used to make a spice vinegar, useful for pickles. For a constant supply of fresh leaves, sow at monthly intervals between March and July. The plants grow up to around 3ft/90cm and have loose heads like fennel and starry yellow flowers.

Paths in the herb garden can be very narrow, just

JUNE

enough to shuffle along to pluck and weed. Brick, laid on edge, always looks satisfying and has a more interesting texture than concrete slabs. Leave the paths as plain beaten earth if the ground is not too sticky.

You may feel the paths define the design sufficiently on their own. If you want stronger lines, outline the beds in either traditional box or in lavender, sage, rosemary or santolina, clipping them close each year. For a taller screen, train sweetbriar (*Rosa eglanteria*) on wires round the plot. It looks like the wild dog rose, but the leaves are hauntingly perfumed, particularly after rain. Chives, pinks and parsley also make good, dense – if impermanent – edging.

1   Mop-head bay
2   Half standard rose
     'The Fairy' or 'Little White Pet'
3   Standard gooseberry
4   Chives
5   Variegated Mint
6   Parsley
7   Woodruff
8   Variegated sage
9   Coriander
10 Sweet Cecily
11 Tarragon
12 Chervil
13 Marjoram
14 Thyme
15 Plain sage
16 Dill
17 Rosemary
18 Comfrey
19 Bergamot

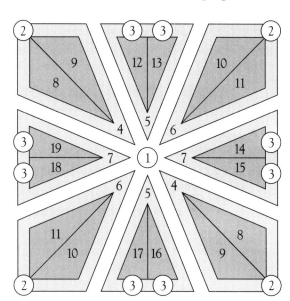

Jobs for the Month

General

❀ The longer the grass, the faster it grows. Mow lawns regularly.

❀ Indoor plants such as azaleas, pelargoniums, ivies and Easter cactus can be set outside until early September.

❀ Herbs such as tarragon and savory can be cut back hard if they are getting straggly. They will soon produce fresh growth.

❀ Pinch out flower heads of chives to increase production of leaf.

❀ Trees and shrubs such as cherries, lilacs, crab apples and medlars normally propagated by grafting may start throwing up suckers from the rootstock. Deal with these quickly.

Flowers

❀ Cut back broom when it has finished flowering, shortening flowered shoots almost to the old wood.

❀ Deadhead lilac.

❀ Cut back *Clematis montana* if it threatens to swamp other plants.

❀ Shear over clumps of aubrieta and arabis to remove dead flower heads.

❀ Cut back *Iris unguicularis* foliage for the sun to warm the rhizomes.

❀ Lift and divide bearded iris that have finished flowering where clumps have become congested. Cut out and throw away bare sections of rhizome and replant the newest pieces.

❀ Cut back weigela after flowering. Each year take out a couple of entire stems down to ground level. Deutzia responds to the same treatment.

❀ Cut back oriental poppy to the ground. This gives its neighbours a chance to cover the space.

❀ Clean up candytuft and alyssum by cutting out flowered stems.

❀ New dahlia plants should be in the ground now, well protected from slugs. Pinch out the tips of young plants to make them bushy. Tie in to strong stakes before growth becomes too heavy.

❀ Stop chrysanthemums set out last month.

❀ If you do not want flowers on your senecio, remove them now.

❀ Mildew can be an unsightly problem in hot, dry summers on roses, acanthus, even pulmonaria. Spray with a proprietary fungicide.

❀ Cut out some of the old branches from shrubs such as *Rubus tridel* 'Benenden' to encourage new growth to form.

❀ Deadhead roses regularly.

❀ Deadhead petunias to keep them blooming prolifically.

🌿 Pick over clumps of violas regularly and deadhead before they set seed.

Vegetables

🌿 Plant outdoor tomatoes, providing each one with a sturdy stake, unless it is one of the sprawling bush varieties. A high-potash feed such as Tomorite helps produce plenty of flowers and fruit. If the plants are short of water, however, too many potash dinners will result in a deficiency of magnesium. Yellowing leaves is usually the first sign of that problem.

🌿 Pinch out the tops of broad bean plants when they have set sufficient pods. The juicy tops are what blackfly most like.

🌿 Leeks can be set out, making deep holes with a dibber and watering a plant into each hole. Space the holes 6in/15cm apart in rows 15in/38cm apart.

🌿 Sow beetroot, carrots and a final row of peas.

🌿 Mulching does a great deal to conserve moisture around thirsty crops such as courgettes, tomatoes and cucumbers.

🌿 Keep onions hand-weeded as they hate competition.

🌿 Hoe carefully between rows of carrots, beetroot and other vegetables.

🌿 Stop cutting asparagus in the middle of the month so that the plants build up some top growth to feed into the roots. Keep asparagus beds clean of weed.

🌿 Collars made from old carpet, underlay or roofing felt will prevent cabbage root flies from having their wicked way with the crop. Cut out circular collars and slit them so that they fit round the stems of cabbages.

Propagating

🌿 Take cuttings of perennial wallflowers. Choose lateral shoots about 2in/5cm long with a heel. Push them into a pot filled with a peat/sand mixture.

🌿 Increase the climbing hydrangea (H. petiolaris) by cuttings of vigorous side shoots.

🌿 Take cuttings of African violets. Pull strong healthy leaves away from the parent plant with about 2in/5cm of stem attached. Sink the stalks into a pot of peat/sand mixture and keep moist and warm (about 65°F/18°C). Pot up the rooted cuttings singly to grow on.

🌿 Stem cuttings of bougainvillea, clianthus, philodendron and stephanotis can also be taken now.

🌿 Take half-ripe cuttings from buddleja, camellia, ceanothus, chaenomeles, choisya, daphne, deutzia, hebe, jasmine, lavatera, philadelphus, weigela.

JULY

Growing a Monet Garden

'My garden is my most beautiful masterpiece,' said the painter Monet about Giverny, his Normandy home, dismissing in a sentence the canvases of haystacks, bridges, rivers, cathedrals and poplars that raise millions of pounds at auction sales.

He moved into the house with his large family in 1883 and stayed until his death 43 years later. During those years he transformed the solidly respectable garden, with its spruce, cypress and tight-clipped hedges of box. Poppies replaced the cabbages; irises and marigolds filled the onion beds. His neighbours were deeply suspicious.

When Monet bought more land on the far side of the road and started to make his famous water garden, suspicion turned to open hostility. Representations were made to the Prefect of the Eure. 'Blow Art. What about our water?' asked the Givernois. Monet pulled rank and strings and got his lily pond. The National Gallery, the Metropolitan Museum in New York, the Musée d'Orsay in Paris and others got their pictures – part of a long series of paintings of the water-lily pond that engaged Monet in the last part of his life.

It was not all plain sailing. The first phase of the great pond project was finished by the autumn of 1893. The famous wooden bridge was built. Willows, alders, bamboos and Japanese cherries were planted, along with quantities of water lilies. Unfortunately, constant traffic on the unsurfaced road between house and water garden kicked up clouds of dust which settled thickly on the water-lily pads. Even *plein-air* painters have their breaking points. Monet paid for the whole of the road alongside the garden to be tarred.

This is all rather reassuring. Gazing at the artist's translucent canvases it is easy to forget that the things that look most effortless usually require the most effort. The tranquil, seemingly timeless lily pond was born out of conflict and hard labour.

Among the Monet jigsaw puzzles, notepads, address books and postcards that armies of helpers will sell you at any Monet exhibition, you sometimes find little collections of seed packets, labelled *Mélange jaune* or *Mélange bleu*. Buy a bit of the Giverny dream, suggests the blurb. Throw them in the wind, it says and asks a high price for the privilege.

If only it were that easy! For the same price you could buy a useful collection of seed from Suttons or Thompson & Morgan, both of which provide clearer instructions on the packet about bringing the seeds to a fruitful birth. Better than a *Mélange rose* (containing morning glory, godetia, gypsophila and carnation, all jumbled up) will be separate packets of pot marigolds, aquilegias, snapdragons and asters, all of which grow in profusion in the narrow flower beds in front of the house at Giverny.

I have never been to Monet's garden, but the photographs and paintings and films that I have seen show something entirely different from the subdued English herbaceous style, more like the splendid bright planting of municipal parks: geometric flower beds with spring spreads of forget-me-nots, punctuated by brilliant red and yellow tulips; summer groups of orange and red dahlias, with quantities of pillarbox pelargoniums.

Studying the planting plans for Monet's garden, you realize that the first step to making your own English Giverny is to jettison all the tasteful schemes of grey, pink and mauve that garden designers lull us with, and dive head-first into colour. Nasturtiums, gladioli, cannas, yellow and orange rudbeckias and sunflowers are the unfashionable flowers we should be looking at.

Profusion – of flowers rather than foliage – is the overwhelming impression from images of Giverny. For this you need a good deal of sun to encourage flowers rather than the lush leafy growth we get with cool damp summers. In a hot summer, Giverny gardens will be all the easier to create here. Pelargoniums can be set out sooner, dahlias will come into flower by July.

Spiky cactus dahlias seemed particularly favoured

by Monet. 'Alva's Doris' would be a good one to try, or 'Cornish Riviera', a blood-red semi-cactus variety with flowers 6in/15cm across. Those who still blench at the thought of a dahlia at close quarters should let themselves in gently with a variety such as 'Christopher Taylor'. If you squint slightly, it looks just like a peony.

The disadvantage of the Giverny style is evident in winter. Monet's pictures show the garden in late spring and high summer. Photographs out of season show empty narrow earth strips, the terrain of a market gardener specializing in asparagus. When the delicious profusion of snapdragons, campanulas and morning glory melts in the first frost, there is not much left to sustain you through the winter. Whether this matters depends on your temperament.

For the authentic Monet look, give yourself a rampant climbing framework of roses and clematis. On the ground, the style depends on two main flushes, spring and summer on the same patch of ground. Snowdrops, aubrietas and jonquils will do the first part of spring, followed by a massive profusion of tulips and *Iris germanica*. Red and yellow tulips seem often to have been planted together, but a rainbow jumble would not be the thing. Buy more of fewer varieties rather than the other way around. Do not stick to the restrained kind. Monet had plenty of mad parrot tulips at Giverny.

JULY

149

The irises, although flowering only for a relatively short period in May, lend strong foliage to the planting scheme for the rest of the season. The true *Iris germanica* is sweetly scented and has rich purplish-blue petals with a white beard. It is early and the foliage is evergreen. Since Monet's death, hybrids of this bearded iris have been raised, notably by Kelways Nursery at Langport, Somerset, which still sells a magnificent selection. In choosing varieties, stick to clear colours for a Giverny garden. 'Langport Chief' is a purple-blue with dark falls, 'Langport Finch' a bright mid-blue. The plants tend to be a little shorter and the flowers larger than on the true *I. germanica*.

For summer choose low-growing *Campanula carpatica* to edge the front of your border, or a tangle of creeping nasturtium. Fill in behind with a bed of snapdragons, interplanted with dahlias. The plans of the flower garden at Giverny, with its masses of small beds separated by raked sand paths, show no room to build up the complicated plant associations of our typical herbaceous borders.

Instead, use asters under clematis with Japanese anemones to take over later in the season. Use pelargoniums with cannas. Plant pinks with dark blue monkshoods to take over later in the season. Use oriental poppies: shear off the foliage when it has died and follow them with brilliant red 'Bishop of Llandaff' dahlias. Shock the neighbours. Monet did.

Scrambling about with Nelly Moser

There is nothing I can say on the subject of clematis that has not already been better said by the master, Christopher Lloyd. If you *really* want to know about these plants, get hold of the latest edition of his book *Clematis*.

Choosing between varieties is the worst task. Pruning clematis is not such a shibboleth once you have grasped the idea that the three different ways of treating them roughly match up with the three different periods of flowering: early, mid-season and late. The late-flowering kinds such as 'Jackmanii Superba', all the *viticella* varieties such as 'Abundance' and 'Royal Velours', and the rose-pink 'Comtesse de Bouchaud' all need cutting back hard in February or March. Stick to these kinds and you need only shear your way once through the clematis maze.

You will miss many of the delights that are in flower earlier, however: creamy white 'Henryi' with stamens the colour of milk chocolate, deep pink 'Bees' Jubilee', striped 'Nelly Moser' and, one of my own favourites, the pale blue 'Mrs Cholmondeley'. All these have their main flush of flowers in late May to June and a reasonable second display at the end of summer. These need only light pruning in late February or March; you should cut out any dead or weak stems and shorten the rest to a strong growth bud.

The third group, mostly early-flowering, needs no pruning at all. The spring-flowering C. *macropetala* varieties belong here ('Markham's Pink', 'Snow-bird'). So do all the C. *montana* types such as 'Elizabeth' and 'Tetrarose'. No April-flowering C. *alpina* variety needs attention. Nor does the even earlier C. *armandii* with large smooth evergreen leaves.

The most important factor is the final resting place of your clematis. If you get it right, this need not be the rubbish heap. By nature, clematis are scramblers; they have no means by which they can stick themselves to supports. They are, however, beautifully equipped for hoisting themselves through some other growing thing and this is how they look best. A clematis plant is not in itself a thing of beauty. It has no particular form. Its flowers are its only *raison d'être*.

As it has naturally evolved as a scrambler, clematis thrives best with its feet in the shade and its head in the sun. Grown through some host such as ceanothus or viburnum, these conditions occur without much effort on your part. 'Mrs Cholmondeley' threading its way through an April-flowering ceanothus will keep decently out of the limelight until the ceanothus has finished its display and then quietly take over a starring role in late May and June. Or you could use the excellent combination of summer ceanothus and the greenish-white C. *florida* 'Alba Plena' flowering together in Christopher Lloyd's book.

These types used in combination need hard pruning, so each year you have a chance to sort out the
tangle of shoots. Half a dozen little interferences in
spring is all it takes to persuade a clematis to range
experimentally over a wide area rather than bunch its
stems altogether in a single matted twist. 'Jackmanii
Superba', an extremely vigorous variety with sumptuous velvety blooms of deep purple, responds particularly well to this gentle nudging. I have it on a south
wall of the house where it wanders among the wisteria. A bush of rue, a peony and other neighbours
prevent the sun from shining too hotly on the clematis roots. A thick mulch of muck in late spring also
provides insulation – and food, for if the clematis is
sharing space with a host shrub, it is also sharing food
and drink. Make sure there is plenty of both.

'Jackmanii Superba' is quite happy with this south
aspect; 'Nelly Moser' would not be. The flowers, pale
mauve with vivid carmine bars running from base to
tip of each petal, fade badly in full sunshine. The
same is true of the similar 'Marcel Moser' and 'Bees'
Jubilee'. These are best on east or west walls, but will
also flower on north-facing walls, provided that they
are not hideously exposed. The elegant white 'Marie
Boisselot' is happy with a sunless north aspect. So is
the pale blue 'Lady Northcliffe'. Pale clematis shine
out in dark corners. Dark purple here would be glum.

Clematis montana provides particular delight (and

dangers). It is magnificently profligate with its small flowers and smells memorably of vanilla. (None of the dinner-plate clematis can summon up any smell.) It needs space, though, and lots of it. It will soon swamp a porch and drown a host shrub. It is lost if thrown casually at an apple tree, for it comes into flower at the same time as the apple blossom. Give it a large, high stump, a shed or expansive wall to play with. It is bad with roofs, since tendrils creep under tiles and felting and prise them out of position.

Nobody has yet raised a large-flowered yellow clematis. The most popular yellows are late-season varieties such as *C. orientalis* and *C. tangutica*, very similar varieties with small cup-shaped flowers made from stiff, thick petals. You could also think of *C. rehderiana*. The flowers are minimal, palest yellow, but the smell is good – cowslips in sun.

Red Alert on the Tomato Front

Hot, dry summers are brilliant for growing outdoor tomatoes. The drought does not seem to worry them. They are, after all, used to it in their native lands. My plants get a fair bit of fussing when they are first planted out and while they are settling in. After that they have to make do with one long drench and a thick mulch of grass cuttings. The crops can be stupendous, with the season stretching from mid-July through to the beginning of November.

I have temporarily abandoned the sort of tomatoes that need staking in favour of bush varieties. They are simplicity itself to manage and the flavour of the new varieties, buffed up by hours of sunshine, is outstanding. Once planted, they can be left entirely to their own devices. You do not have to pinch out side shoots or tie any stems in to canes. The plants start to sag gently as they grow and then sprawl around on the ground, popping out fruit as fast as children with bubble gum.

In greenhouses, whitefly are the chief irritation around tomatoes. With these outdoor bush types, small black slugs are the chief nuisance, for they come out in the evenings like wine-tasters – a nibble here, a nibble there, nothing properly consumed, but a good deal started. I use pellets if they get too greedy.

Over the last few years, there has been a massive boom in new varieties of outdoor bush tomato. The first outdoor types were unpopular because they started fruiting so late. If the weather was miserable, they did not fruit at all. Using the smaller types of cherry tomato such as 'Gardener's Delight' and 'Sub-Arctic' as parents, breeders have come up with a magnificent race of fast-maturing varieties such as 'Red Alert' and 'Tornado'. The taste, to anyone more used to cotton-wool 'Alicante', is a revelation.

Last year I experimented with two trial varieties, 'Tumbler' and 'Ostona'. 'Tumbler' is bred by the same man that came up with 'Red Alert'. The plants raised from seed sown in the third week of March were stringier, less leafy than most other varieties I have grown, but once put out, they grew phenomenally, branching from the main stem and leaping to the business of making trusses of flowers, all of which set well. It was two and a half weeks earlier to fruit than 'Ostona' and more generous with its crops than 'Red Alert'. The fruit are larger than 'Gardener's Delight'.

Suttons suggest using it in a hanging basket. Its habit certainly suits it for this treatment, but I would not expect it to crop as heavily in a basket or any other container of that size as it does in open ground. In a hot dry summer, feeding and watering would also be more problematic in a hanging basket. In the open ground, if you have been looking after your soil properly, tomatoes do not need bottle-feeding.

Because they look quite pretty (even more so if you wind them round with canary creeper or some such extra) and because they will fit into tubs and grow-bags, tomatoes are a popular crop to grow. They have had a lot of ground to make up in the last fifty years. When they were first introduced, they were looked on with great suspicion, possibly because they are members of the same family (Solanaceae) as the poisonous deadly nightshade. The first tomatoes that the old world saw were yellow ones, christened '*pomo d'oro*' by the Italians. They are still about, but they do not fruit as heavily as the red ones.

In England, where they appeared towards the end of the sixteenth century, they were long known as love apples. They are still listed under that name in Johnson's *Gardeners' Dictionary*, a splendid book published in 1886. Whereas Johnson had no problem in filling five columns of his dictionary with a paeon of praise for the pea, he seemed still uncertain about the tomato. It got one grudging column.

In another manual of the same period, Beeton's *Shilling Gardening*, there are two illustrations of tomatoes. One is captioned 'Good Type of Yellow Tomato', the other, an entirely similar fruit, 'Good Type of Red Tomato'. Since they are both black and white engravings, there is little you can learn here. Johnson talks vaguely about the Common Large, the pear-shaped and cherry tomatoes. There were evidently no named varieties. Although glasshouses were in their heyday when both these old encyclopaedias were written, neither author suggests growing the tomato as a greenhouse crop.

With outdoor tomatoes, there is nothing to be gained by sowing seed too soon, since plants cannot go outside until all danger of frost is past. The middle or end of March is early enough. Last year I sowed 'Tornado' on 14 April; consequently it started fruiting later than the other two types I grew and this suited me fine.

Cover the seed thinly with compost when you sow and keep the pot moist in a temperature around 65°F/18°C. When the seedlings have grown their first pair of proper leaves, pot them on, growing each plant singly in a 3in/7.5cm pot. If you want only a few plants, you can sow two or three seeds direct into a small pot, thinning out the weakest seedlings as they develop. Harden them off gradually before planting them out. If they catch cold, their leaves go blue.

'Ostona', one of the trial varieties I grew, was bred specifically to put up with low temperatures. Even if this characteristic is not put to the test, it crops heavily and the tomatoes are sweet.

You can get 'Tumbler' from Suttons and they say that it succeeds well in grow-bags. As it grows low and bushy, you can do without the clothes-horse props you generally need as supports. Try one plant in a deep 14in/35cm hanging basket.

The excellent 'Tornado', from Marshalls, has slightly larger fruit than 'Gardener's Delight' types, with no loss of flavour. Set plants 2ft/30cm apart. 'Red Alert' is available from Unwins, the Henry Doubleday Research Association and elsewhere. Expect about six pounds of fruit from a plant. You will get about 20 tomatoes in each pound.

The most eclectic selection of tomatoes comes

from Robinson's. They have 'Yellow Currant', 'Yellow Pear' and 'Round Yellow' as well as the patriotic 'Britain's Breakfast'. These should be grown on single stems, with the side shoots pinched out.

They are one of the few crops that you can scarcely have too much of. They freeze well and although the texture of the fruit disintegrates in the process, the taste remains very good. The easiest way to prepare them is to do nothing. Just bag them up as they are. They stay whole and separate like marbles rolling round in a bag. This is a huge advantage when you want to use them. You do not have to hack and bash away at a solid frozen mass to extract your half-pound.

When you run each frozen tomato under the tap, the skin slips off like a silk camisole. I am enormously grateful to the person who told me this. Until then, I had been peeling tomatoes before freezing. With small tomatoes, as most bush types are, this is a time-consuming business.

Ripe home-grown tomatoes will sit happily on the plant for two weeks or more. They are certainly better there than in the fridge, which does them no good at all. Green leftover fruit generally get made into chutney.

Some bossy recipes instruct you to get rid of the seeds before you use tomatoes for cooking. A high concentration of vitamins lies in the jelly coating of these seeds. It seems a pity to waste them.

I'm Dreaming of an Earthenware Pitcher

Only affluence could spawn such a conceit as the Cottage Garden Society. It is the same affluence that has made the magazine *Country Living* such a spectacular success. Yet 49 per cent of *Country Living*'s readers live in London. A large proportion of the other half pilot their Volvos round the congested streets of Winchester, Bath and other urban centres. The country dream is potent, and certainly more comfortable than the reality.

Any day now I expect to come across a lovingly compiled photo essay on the paint finishes of old cottage privies. I cannot remember much about the paint finishes – only the freezing cold, the damp and the torn pages of *Farmers' Weekly* spiked on a hazel stick. I knew a lot about corn prices as a child.

Nostalgia is an odd disease, but not an exclusively modern one. The Victorian watercolours of Helen Allingham and Myles Birket Foster, painted in a time of intense rural deprivation, represent the apotheosis of the cottage idyll: plenty of hollyhocks, roses tumbling round the door, smiling babies, the odd kitten gambolling in a spare bit of foreground. No mud.

Allingham, born in 1848, studied painting in Birmingham and at the Royal Academy Schools. In 1874 she married the poet William Allingham and they lived for seven years in Chelsea. In 1881 the couple moved to Sandhills, near Witley in Surrey, where, William recorded in his diary, Helen was 'diligent at her cottages'. Seven years later they left Surrey for the sanctuary of Hampstead, where Helen stayed for the rest of her life. This pattern has been repeated many times since. Idylls are so much easier when reality is not staring you in the face.

Sixty of Allingham's paintings appeared in 1909 in *The Cottage Homes of England*, written by Stewart Dick. 'Her cottages have always a green and smiling old age,' he pointed out. 'The garden is full of flowers, the sun shines with a cool and tempered light and the whole scene breathes of peacefulness. There is no jarring note.'

In the modern idyll the cottage of course will be discreetly electrified and plumbed, though we do not want to think too much about that side of things. It is more nourishing to dwell on earthenware pitchers and bunches of lavender hung from the rafters.

The cottage dream is also bound up with the Pre-Raphaelite ideal of a perfect community. Neighbours will smile benignly as you pass; they will not play loud music at two o'clock in the morning. But the dream could never encompass the people that actually filled my own post-war country childhood: the man with the enormous goitre on his neck, the farmer at Chapel Mill who raged and threw stones at us whenever we, or anyone else, passed by, the man we

JULY

called Mussolini who lived on the side of the mountain in a cottage called Valley View. Whitewash was his thing. He whitewashed whole trees, stones in the lane, his hedge, his chicken house. He made a very small whitewashed gate in the hedge and a whitewashed sign that hung above saying 'Valley View. Chickens Only'.

Given the reality, it is one of the ironies of gardening that the cottage style is so in vogue with affluent thirty-somethings. It is now a matter of artifice – planting certain flowers, buying certain seats, making assemblages of watering cans and wicker baskets.

The true cottage garden is completely without artifice, its layout and contents dictated mostly by necessity. Paths are straight and purposeful. For the real cottager, the best way to the front door is the shortest. Only those playing at shepherdesses can afford the luxury of the scenic route.

In real cottage gardens, vegetables take up most of the ground. Mussolini's garden, on a fine south-facing slope, was productively filled with kale and cabbage, leeks, potatoes, turnips, parsnips, carrots and beans, all luckily too evanescent to qualify for the whitewash treatment. There was no poncing about with flowers.

If vegetables find a place in the modern, stylized cottage garden, they will as likely as not have been planted for their looks rather than their economic worth. We can afford the luxury of feeding the soul.

162

This to some extent explains the success of the Cottage Garden Society. Pat Taylor, the publicity officer, joined when she came down to Cheshire from Scotland. She had always had rhododendrons, suddenly found herself in a cottage with a derelict garden and wanted to know what to do with it. Some keen gardeners join because of the seed list distributed each year to members. It is strong on traditional cottage garden flowers, such as aquilegias, hollyhocks, campanulas, foxgloves, irises, sweet peas and poppies.

Some members, as one would suspect, do not have gardens at all, but like the outings and the newsletter. 'To read about sweet violets and the first snowdrops and all that sort of thing,' says Mrs Taylor. The Society is pragmatic in its view of the cottage garden. 'We don't pretend we're in a time warp or worry too much about historical accuracy in the flowers we grow. It's more about a way of doing things.'

It is impossible to reproduce the artlessness with which the true cottage gardens were made, but it is not difficult to create a pastiche, provided you don't try to get too clever. The overall design should be simple and linear – perhaps two paths dividing a plot into four squares or rectangles – and the planting composed from stalwarts such as campanulas, peonies, pinks and roses.

Against the house walls plant jasmine, both summer and winter kinds, some old blowzy rose and a

fruit tree, perhaps trained into a geometric espalier shape. Edge paths with a fringing of chives, the little double daisy *Bellis perennis*, old-fashioned pinks or small violas.

Roses in the cottage garden will not be hybrid teas, but something altogether more wayward. One of the musks would do, or a form of the ancient *Rosa alba*. Moss roses would also be at home. They are not as popular now as with the Victorians, who had about forty varieties to choose from. Some are prone to mildew. 'Common Moss' is a well-mossed pink with a good smell. The simpler the name, the more likely a flower is to fit into a reconstructed cottage plot.

Plant herbs and flowers that knock you out with their scent. Lilies of the valley were traditionally planted in the dank area around the outside privy, but are equally happy in similar conditions round a toolshed. Use wallflowers, evening primroses and mezereon, which is swathed from February to April with scented purple flowers that you can smell even through the worst of colds.

Above all, relax. Proper cottagers could not afford the luxury of agonizing over the exact shade of blue for their campanulas; nor should you. If you try too hard, you will have lost the point. Give the plants their heads. Cottage gardens as often as not work best because of something you didn't do, rather than something you did.

JOBS FOR THE MONTH

General

🌿 Gather herbs such as rosemary and thyme hang them to dry in a cool, airy place.

🌿 Trim hedges regularly – especially if they are privet. Untended hedges tend to become bare at the base.

Flowers

🌿 Cut down flowered stems of aquilegia and sweet rocket before they seed.

🌿 Continue to deadhead roses.

🌿 Keep picking sweet peas. They will stop flowering if they are allowed to run to seed.

🌿 Sow Brompton stocks, pansies and perennial poppies in seed beds outside now for flowering next year.

🌿 Cut out flowered stems from mock orange (*Philadelphus coronarius*), leaving the new shoots to flower next season.

🌿 Continue to deadhead violas to encourage them to produce new flowers. Clumps that have got very leggy can be sheared down close to the ground.

🌿 Wisterias need two prunings in a year. Do the first now, the second in February. First choose the growths that you want to keep to fill extra space and if they have not started twining round any sup-port, help them on their way. Shorten all other growths, leaving five or six pairs of leaves intact.

🌿 Start to plant autumn-flowering bulbs such as colchicum and sternbergia.

🌿 Cut back helianthemums.

🌿 Delphiniums may give a second late show if you cut down the first stems as soon as they have finished flowering.

🌿 If evergreen ceanothus has grown out too far from a wall, prune back flowered sprays to a few buds from the main branch.

🌿 For the biggest dahlias, take off the two side buds that generally appear on either side of the central boss bud.

🌿 Gather fresh seed from astrantia, cam-panula, foxglove, hollyhock, honesty, hellebore and polemonium.

🌿 Pinch out the tips of home-grown wallflowers to make plants bushy and compact.

🌿 Regular deadheading extends displays in pots and hanging baskets. Pay particu-lar attention to ageratum, marigolds, cornflowers and pansies.

Vegetables

🌿 Support runner beans with poles.

🌿 Transplant cabbages and broccoli from seed bed to final position while the ground is still damp.

🌱 Thin kohlrabi plants so that they are not less than 6in/15cm apart.

🌱 Thin young beetroot.

🌱 Sow more lettuce and radish for continuity. If the weather is dry, water the seed drill before you sow.

🌱 Transplant purple sprouting broccoli, setting the young plants deeper in the soil than they had been in the seed bed. Water them liberally into the holes and then firm down the earth hard.

🌱 Lift garlic as soon as the leaves begin to wither and allow the bulbs to ripen on netting outside as you would onions. Clean them off and hang up in bunches.

🌱 Lift early potatoes as the haulms begin to die down.

Fruit

🌱 Leave the two strongest runners on each strawberry plant and nip out the rest. When the season has finished, tidy up beds by cutting off old leaves and removing straw.

🌱 Pick whitecurrants and redcurrants regularly.

🌱 Apple and pear trees trained in espaliers, cordons and fans may need summer pruning. Do this gradually, so the tree does not suffer a shock.

🌱 Cut out old raspberry canes as soon as fruiting has finished. Tie in eight or ten new canes to each plant.

🌱 Prune stone fruit such as plums and cherries: cut out diseased and dead branches and thin out over-vigorous growth.

🌱 Plant new strawberry plants, setting them at least 15in/38cm apart in rows 2½ft/75cm apart.

Propagating

🌱 Take 3in/75mm cuttings of pinks and root them in pots of peat and sand.

🌱 Take cuttings from cistus, using non-flowering side shoots.

🌱 Layer border carnations. Choose young side shoots that have not flowered and nick through the joint at the base. Bend the side shoots down and peg them to the ground. Cover the stem with fine, damp soil and keep well watered. The layers should root by early September.

🌱 Increase hybrids such as loganberry and tayberry by tip layering. Bury a shoot tip about 6in/15cm in the ground and firm down the earth. By next spring it should be well rooted.

🌱 Layer azaleas, choosing shoots growing close to the ground. Make a nick with a sharp knife on the underside. Scrape out a hollow in the ground and bury each branch in its own little trench, pinned down with bent wire.

AUGUST

Monstrous Weeds

Rain is wonderful for weeds. Docks grow to tropical proportions and you can wring enough water to wash in from the crunchy stems of sow thistles. You might suppose that all the time spent watering in a drought year could be switched to attacking the weeds that profit by another year's wet. Somehow it doesn't work out like that.

In a grudging way, you have to admire the cheek of weeds. Without an invitation, they turn up anyway to the party and then proceed to take it over, elbowing out the delicate flower aesthetes who had gathered for an intellectual discussion of colour and texture.

They remind you how thin the skim is of garden over wilderness. Weeds were here first, and they don't want you to forget it. Turn your back and they creep silently back into their territory, garrotting the newcomers as they advance.

I have got a new weed in my garden – enchanter's nightshade (*Circaea lutetiana*). You can almost fool plant snobs with it. It has the minimalist flowers beloved of the most refined gardeners and if you call it by its proper name, it sounds suitably well-bred and obscure.

It's not more than about a foot high with round-stalked, ovate leaves, deeply veined and slightly washed over with red at the margins. Below ground it is a monster. Each stem that you pull up has at least five thick juicy white running roots, as brittle as rice paper. It seems to favour damp, shady places and had completely crowded out a colony of variegated gingermint, no mean street fighter itself.

A determined weeding session liberated a bed about 30ft/10m long by 10ft/3m wide. There is a fragile truce now, but I can almost hear those snapped off bits of underground root plotting insurrection.

Underground runners are the sneakiest of weeds, and the most difficult to get rid of. Miraculously, the garden did not have ground elder in it when we first arrived, but it's here now, brought in, I would imagine, on the roots of herbaceous perennials such as golden rod and michaelmas daisy that people always seem to have available to give away in suspiciously large quantities.

These days, I put everything of that nature into a quarantine bed first, to see what bombs are lurking unseen in the tangle of root and earth. Creeping thistle is another horror that often arrives in the roots of other plants.

Annual weeds are not so sinister. There are plenty of them, but they do not represent a serious threat. They are profligate, though. Fat hen, one of the commonest weeds of arable land, with succulent leaves and heads of small, bobbly green flowers, can carry up to 28,000 seeds on one plant. Most common weeds, such as groundsel or annual meadow grass, produce at least 500 seeds each.

Thick planting is the best way to beat annual weeds among flowers. In the vegetable garden, hoeing brings them to heel, a job made easier if you plant in straight lines rather than broadcast seed. *Gardening from Which?* reported that black plastic was the most efficient and cost-effective weed suppressor in their trials, but I would prefer any day to look at a thumpingly healthy sow thistle than sterile plastic.

The great thing is to catch annual weeds before they seed, which most of them do in August. That is their only aim in life. Mulches of grass or ground bark are effective, where they are appropriate, but they have to be thick. Weed seeds germinate in the top 2in/5cm of soil. The mulch needs to be thicker than that.

Areas of soft fruit, currants and gooseberries respond well to the mulching routine. So does our dahlia bed, now just exploding into flower. Unfortunately, this way of managing things favours my ancient enemy, bindweed, which snakes around just under the surface of the mulch, fattening itself in this warm, moist bed.

After one whinge about bindweed, someone suggested planting honeysuckle next to it: 'It disappears at the drop of a hat.' I think my advisor meant the bindweed. Unfortunately I already had ghastly evidence that the remedy would not be effective. One of my honeysuckles, *Lonicera tellmanniana*, draped over a stump, is riddled with bindweed and since the two of them twine together like strands in a rope, it is a complicated job getting rid of it.

I do not want to use weedkiller here, but am not averse to using it in some parts of the garden, always for a specific purpose. Weedkiller comes into its own when we are breaking new ground, subduing the impenetrable tangle of growth that covers the bank, which I am gradually planting up.

It takes about three years to get a piece of ground clean enough to plant in, to get rid of bad, perennial weeds. After that, I don't dig, but plant direct into the ground, using a thick underlay of perennials to stop weeds spreading under new trees and shrubs.

Glyphosate (Murphy's Tumbleweed) is one of the most efficient herbicides for this job. It kills whatever it touches – which makes it dicy to use among plants you want to keep – but it is a non-persistent weedkiller. It doesn't hang around contaminating the soil. It kills top growth relatively slowly – you don't see the results for about a month – but it is a translocated herbicide. It works through the leaves of a plant down to its roots, which it also kills. You can use it any time that weeds are growing, though it is most effective when there is the maximum leaf area to take it in. Docks and nettles are best bashed just as they are coming into flower.

You can also eat nettles, which is a very satisfactory way of dealing with them. It makes you feel like a cannibal, consuming his enemy so as to be strengthened by him. By summer there are plenty of other vegetables around, and nettle leaves are coarse and bitter. But in spring, when there's a dearth of fresh greens, the tops of young nettles make a delicious purée, a bit like spinach and equally good for the haemoglobin. The recipe I use is Anton Mosimann's. Peel and dice a small potato and put it in a large saucepan with 8oz/250g of nettle tops. Add ¾pt/450ml stock and simmer for 20 minutes. Drain the nettles well and purée them. Season with salt, pepper and lots of nutmeg and beat in 3–4oz/about 100g of fromage blanc or soft goat's cheese. Reheat gently.

Does anyone have an equally good recipe for bindweed?

~·⊗·~

A POT-BOUND PLOT

Small is a matter of opinion, as a city gardening club once found at a lecture given by one of the Rothschilds. 'No garden, however small,' he began, 'should be without its acre of woodland.' However you look at it though, the garden at 41 Beaumont

Road, St Judes, Plymouth, in Devon, is *really* small.

The house is in the middle of an 1870s terrace. All originally had gardens about 15ft/5m wide and 60ft/18m long. At No. 41, the length has been nibbled at from both ends. Its owners, Alan and Eileen Parsons, built on an extension to their kitchen which gobbled up one large chunk. At the other end is a garage. This leaves a space 8ft/2.5m long for the garden. A narrow passage, known as camellia alley, runs the whole length of the right-hand boundary.

The most extraordinary thing about the garden is that nearly everything, including the forty camellias, at least as many clematis, abies, hydrangea, pieris, lapageria, roses and crinodendron, grows in pots. Small pots sit balanced on top of the earth in bigger pots. Brackets hold pots against the walls, so that banks of plants are built up on top of each other. Big butchers' 'S' hooks hold hanging baskets where pots cannot be fitted in. The range of plants that the Parsons grow would be impressive in a garden four times the size. Here it is astonishing.

From time to time, plants outgrow the yard and are handed on to friends who have what Alan calls 'pukka' gardens. Occasionally a plant seems to tire of pot life and begins to flag. If it does not pick up after a session in the recovery ward (the garage roof, where there is space and light), it too is pensioned off in some place where it can get its roots into real earth.

AUGUST

The surprising thing is how few plants object to the constraints placed on them.

Little repotting is ever done. Many of the plants are too big to handle in this way. Others have become so intertwined with their neighbours that they could never be disentangled for a repotting job. The Parsons use a loam-based John Innes compost for most of their plants. It is heavier than peat-based composts and gives the pots stability. Lighter peat composts are used in the hanging baskets, made up three times a year with winter, spring and summer displays. In winter there may be fleshy-leaved bergenias interplanted with ipheion, or a selection of different ivies. In summer, scented-leaved pelargoniums and fuchsias are brought into play.

Any intensive form of gardening, such as this, depends on having an area where plants can be rested, or brought on before facing the limelight outside. In the Parsons' case, this is the garage, as it is still called. Eileen Parsons treats it more like a conservatory. She persuaded her husband to replace the solid roof with sheets of Perspex, so that the interior is extremely light. He still hangs on grimly to a space inside that is the size of a very small car. The rest of the place is crammed with plants.

On the right-hand side is a workbench, a sort of potting station, overflowing with cuttings, seedlings and plants waiting for their turn in the hanging baskets. On the left-hand side is a tropical section with tubs of arums, some all white, some extremely handsome with enormous leaves and spathes splashed with green (*Zantedeschia* 'Green Goddess'). A cream-coloured clematis with purple stamens, C. *florida bicolor*, rambles towards the roof struts. Waxy hoya meets it on the other side, and an exotic tender fuchsia with enormous bunches of deep red flowers, F. *boliviana*, cascades down from what was once Alan Parsons' tool store.

'Things are not growing in any special system here,' said Mrs Parsons unnecessarily, waving a vague arm over jasmine, aeoniums and plumbago. 'I think of this as a space to have fun, to experiment.' 'I still think of it as a garage,' said her husband, eyebrows signalling furiously.

From the extended kitchen at the back of the house you would not know that this building was a garage, for it is completely smothered in plants. The only bit that isn't is filled with a small lean-to greenhouse, more of a glass cupboard, just big enough to get your arms into.

A long piece of mirror on the left-hand side, veiled with ironwork and masked by plants, gives the impression that the garden goes on very much farther than it does. Pieris, variegated pittosporum, nandina, golden robinia and the handsome *Abies koreana* provide a rich and varied foliage background in and out of which tumble roses, clematis, lilies and tropaeolum.

In a black industrial polypropylene bucket by the back door grows a superbly healthy *Rhododendron yakushimanum*, its narrow, dark leaves backed with a thick layer of russet coloured felt. The advantage of growing plants in containers is that each can be given the mixture it likes best. The rhododendron is grow-ing in an acid, ericaceous compost. You don't notice the bucket, but Alan Parsons would like to broadcast the fact that they make good tough long-lasting con-tainers, with half a dozen holes bored through the bottom. Ordinary plastic pots become brittle after a few years. The buckets do not and are lighter to handle than clay pots. Feeding is a regular routine; Tomorite for the camellias every ten days from early spring until July. Feeding any later would encourage soft, sappy growth that would be susceptible to winter draughts.

One camellia, 'Elegans', brought from the Parsons' former garden in Surrey, has been in a pot for twenty-five years. Vine weevil is their worst enemy, especi-ally now that the only effective control – Aldrin – has been withdrawn from the market. They find that drenching pots with diluted Jeyes fluid is some help.

Division of labour in this remarkably labour-intensive matchbox is amicably arranged. 'I think of myself as the experimenter, the architect,' says she.

'I am the financial adviser,' says he. She plants. He prunes. 'Organized chaos,' says she, gazing benignly down camellia alley, with Solomon's seal, senecio and pyracantha threatening to seize up the passageway once and for all. 'Four-star chaos,' says he, wedging some pots of hosta 'Blue Boy', 'Blue Wedgwood' and 'Golden Prayers' more firmly into the top of another pot containing a big golden maple.

'I suppose you've given up buying plants now?' I asked, looking round the bulging yard. 'What a silly question,' Alan Parsons replied. Eileen Parsons directed my gaze to the roof. There are good plants in this garden, well used. Go and see them. Visitors still have a chance of squeezing in between them: the garden is open regularly under the National Gardens Scheme.

⋘⊛⋙

From Boudoir to Hanging Basket

There is too much of the boudoir about the fuchsia for it ever to be one of my favourite flowers. Struggling, however, for a proper impartiality, I visited Stuart Lockyer, who grows 500 different varieties in his nursery outside Bristol.

Mr Lockyer was not a happy man when I saw him. His max/min thermometer was once again registering a temperature in the high 90s – the mid 30s centigrade. Fuchsias like moseying along somewhere in the middle 60s F – around 18–19°C. The nursery greenhouses are shaded, ventilated, irrigated, but still there had been deaths. Plant roots had not been able to take up moisture as fast as the leaves were losing it up above.

Some varieties were coping better than others. Between his groans, Mr Lockyer noticed that of all his charges, the *triphylla* hybrids minded the heat least. These include varieties such as 'Thalia' and 'Gartenmeister Bonstedt' which have crept away from the boudoir towards the gypsy encampment. The leaves are larger than most fuchsias', darker too, with a lustrous, bronze finish. The long thin flowers, more orange than magenta, are held in clusters at the tips of the stems. The *triphyllas* are very tender and must be brought inside for the winter.

The other thing Mr Lockyer noticed was that pale-flowered varieties suffered more than dark, which might be worth bearing in mind if you are stocking a conservatory. Fuchsias do not like blazing sun. If you grow them in pots outside, a position facing north is as good as any. They will get a splash of sun at the fag ends of the day and will not cook meantime.

If you are planting hardy varieties in a border, then a position in dappled shade, but not overhung, will please them. A soil that is neutral or the tiniest bit on the acid side (pH 6.5) is said to suit them best, but I grow them on soil that is markedly more alkaline than that and they do not seem to mind.

For growing in pots Mr Lockyer prefers what he calls a peaty John Innes. He mixes his own compost, of course, and includes, always, 20 per cent of loam in his mix. For established plants, you will need a compost such as John Innes No. 3. You will also need to feed regularly. What did Mr Lockyer recommend? I asked. Why, he replied, his own, his very own Fu-Feed for Fabulous Fuchsias. The feed is packed as tight as a warhead with nitrogen and potash and, used once a week, will result in a suitably explosive spate of flowers.

Where tolerance of cold is concerned, fuchsias can be roughly sorted into one of three groups. The fussiest are the *triphyllas*, as I've said; some cascading types such as 'Mantilla', 'Miss California' and 'Lassie', and some of the species such as *Fuchsia boliviana* and *F. fulgens gesneriana*.

The bulk of the varieties fall into the half-hardy class. In sheltered areas of the south-west and possibly in well protected town gardens, these may overwinter outside, but the standard procedure is to bring them inside a greenhouse or conservatory once the first frosts have come and keep them there until spring.

The last and most useful group can be planted out and left out. This includes the well known old variety 'Mrs Popple', raised in 1899, scarlet tube and sepals,

corolla (or petals) dark violet; the low, compact variety 'Alice Hoffmann' with tube and sepals of rose contrasting with a white corolla, and 'Doctor Foster' with scarlet tube and sepals and a vivid corolla of rich violet veined with red – another old variety.

The second half of the nineteenth century was a time of fuchsia mania. The parallel passion for conservatories fuelled an explosion in hybridization. James Lye, gardener at Cliffe Hall, Devizes, was the fuchsia king of the time and some of his varieties are still about. 'Amy Lye' has waxy white tube and sepals and a distinctly orange corolla. 'Lye's Unique' is a strong, upright grower with similarly coloured flowers. These are the varieties I would choose if I lived in a Victorian house, trained perhaps as pillars to stand in pots on either side of the front door.

Fuchsias are most amenable to training. You can persuade them to become lollipop standards, or have them weeping out of urns and hanging baskets. With patience you can make them into pillars or pyramids. It is easier to work with a plant rather than against it. For hanging baskets, choose a naturally cascading variety rather than an upright grower. Mr Lockyer recommends 'Anna of Longleat', 'Australia Fair', 'Balkonkönigin', 'Bicentennial', 'Cascade', 'Crackerjack' and 'La Campanella' – and that is just from the first half of the catalogue. Five plants will fill a 12in/30cm basket. Plant it up early in the season so that the fuchsias are well established and growing away before you put the basket on display. Gradually harden off by putting the basket outside in a shaded, sheltered place by day and bringing it in at night.

Standards require a little more work. Choose varieties such as 'Celia Smedley', 'Checkerboard', 'Marin Glow', 'Snowcap' or 'Tennessee Waltz' with naturally strong upright growth. Tie the stem to a cane and train it up, pinching out any side shoots that may develop in the leaf axils in the main stem. Make ties every 2in/5cm to clamp the growing stem to its stake, otherwise drunken kinks will develop.

As roots fill available space in the pot, transfer the plant to a pot one size larger. When the main stem is about 2½ft/75cm tall, pinch out the growing tip to encourage side shoots to develop at the head. Pinch out the growing tips of these when two or three leaves have developed to encourage yet more side shoots to make a thick, bushy head. When the head is well developed, strip all the leaves from the main stem.

Overwintering fuchsias is the most taxing thing you will have to do with them. In reasonable winters, hardy fuchsias should come through with little fussing. Cut down the stems in late spring rather than autumn as they provide some protection against wind and frost. In exposed areas, hump peat or cinders over the base of the plant for extra insulation.

Half-hardy fuchsias are trickier to manage. First of

all they will need cutting back by about two-thirds. If you have a conservatory or greenhouse that you can keep frost-free through the winter, bring potted fuchsias inside and overwinter them undisturbed, in a temperature of around 40°F/5°C. The soil should be just damp enough to keep the plants ticking over. If you have no place to store them, half-hardies will survive a standard British winter buried in soil, but there must be at least 9in/23cm of earth on top of the root ball. A layer of straw on top, anchored with more soil, further improves insulation.

Winter is no problem for Mr Lockyer who, godlike, can control light, heat, food, drink and bend even the fussiest fuchsia to his will.

<hr />

THE TROPICS OF HORSHAM

Full of nostalgia for rampageous plants after spending some time in the tropics, I went to visit Angus White, proprietor of the extraordinary nursery Architectural Plants. I found him hosing down a magnificent collection of spiky exotica arranged in front of a tin-roofed, wooden-verandahed office, the whole scene straight out of the Caribbean. In leafy Nuthurst, not far from Horsham in West Sussex, this is a clever trick to pull off.

The first thing that needs to be said about Angus

White is that he grows superb plants. His nursery is state of the art and his propagator is Peter Tindley, who for twenty-five years ran the Temperate Nursery at the Royal Botanic Gardens, Kew.

When you buy your plants, you will be told, whether you like it or not, exactly how they were propagated and when, where the plant lives in the wild and what conditions it demands in this country. Sometimes, if it is on public view, you will also be told where the parent plant is growing, so that you can go and check what your progeny will look like when full grown. His *Magnolia delavayi*, for instance, were grown from the fine tree in the walled garden at Borde Hill, Sussex. In an age dominated by garden centres, where the only thing about your plant you will be told with any certainty is the price, this is a miraculous state of affairs.

White's ambition is modest: to own the best run and most interesting nursery in the history of the universe. He is worldly and slightly raffish. There are enough episodes in his past life that he prefers not to discuss to suggest that his has been a youth well misspent. 'Just another long-haired nut,' he says dismissively, leaving you with half-finished threads of his life dangling in California, Hawaii and the back streets of Brighton, where for some time he was lucratively engaged in making antique furniture.

Gardening crept up on him relatively late, but with

a vengeance – not gardening in general, but certain plants in particular. One day he sat down to make a list of them. They were all evergreen exotic plants whose shape and overall presence were more important than any fleeting diversion such as flowers. The same plants later provided the nucleus of his nursery stock and are the ones marked in his catalogue as essential. 'If you want the extraordinary exotic effects that can be created with our plants,' he writes in the foreword to his trendy long, thin catalogue, 'you need to be ruthlessly uncompromising in your selection. To this end, the plants described as essential are ESSENTIAL.'

The new exoticists, as White terms the adventurous and slightly reckless gardeners most likely to understand what he is doing, must therefore have certain key plants in their collection. *Podocarpus salignus* is the standardbearer for the movement, luxuriant, evergreen, tropical in effect – 'utterly beautiful' in White's eyes, a tree that will eventually reach 35ft/11m in a favoured location, with drooping branches and long narrow bright grey-green leaves.

New exoticists, of course, cannot live in the chillier, more exposed parts of Britain. Appropriately sybaritic locations in the south and west, protected town gardens or frost-free conservatories are the places where White's plants will thrive and he is scrupulously honest about this in his catalogue.

'Greenhouse effect?' he says. 'Lead me to it.'

All his plants are sorted into one of three categories. Red labels signify the most dangerous: wonderful Mexican agaves, tropical daturas, spiky puyas from the Andes, velvety-leaved tibouchinas from Brazil. Although they may spend their summers in pots outside, they need protection in winter.

Most of White's shrubs are labelled orange or green. Sensibly sited, he says, a phrase that begs a multitude of questions, the orange range should be hardy throughout southern England. Many have been propagated from parent plants that have come through harsh winters in the past.

Here you will find *Corokia × virgata*, a New Zealand evergreen shrub with white felted leaves and yellow flowers followed by brilliant orange fruit, and the fabulous *Weinmannia trichosperma*, 'one of the top five,' says White, a small Chilean tree with complicated pinnate leaves, as lacy as a fern's.

The rest of the plants are labelled green – hardy anywhere in Britain below 1,000ft/300m. Here was my favourite hydrangea, *H. sargentiana*, with great paddle-shaped leaves of sharkskin, and the sweet-smelling autumn-flowering shrub *Osmanthus armatus*.

A blackboard fills one wall of the potting area covered with reassuringly simple headings invented by himself and Peter Tindley. 'Difficult to wean,' reads one, with two recalcitrant oaks listed underneath. 'Sudden death,' is another, relating to the lime-hating lomatias and fiery embothriums. 'Mealy bug' has a distressingly long list attached, including phormium, albizia and echeveria.

I was immensely cheered by all this. It indicated a nursery where people are in close contact with plants and where individual quirks are quickly picked up and catered for. I am also excited by the possibilities that these handsome plants conjure up, although my credentials for belonging to any movement calling itself the new exoticists are shaky.

I like the idea of creating a small courtyard garden, theatrical in the extreme, with huge-leaved tetra-panax, one of the most dramatic of White's plants, looming out of one corner and the scalloped leaves of the Japanese cartwheel tree (*Trochodendron aralioides*) whirling around in another. I would grow agaves and yuccas and succulent aeoniums, hopelessly frost-prone, but they at least could be whisked in their pots under cover in winter if necessary. On White's reckoning, the rest would survive.

I like even better the idea of building a conserva-tory (I am always going on about this) – not one of those glassed-in sitting rooms that designers call conservatories, but a real palace for plants. I would fill it dangerously to the brim with White's red-label specials. That would see me through the grey winter days very happily, drunk on dreams of the tropics.

JOBS FOR THE MONTH

General

⚘ Trim evergreen hedges such as holly and yew and reshape topiary if necessary. If you trim too late, new growth is knocked back by frost.

⚘ In sultry, overcast weather, top up the water in pools to bring much-needed oxygen to gasping fish. Thin out pond weeds if growth becomes too dense.

⚘ This is a good time to prepare sites for new lawns to be sown next month.

⚘ Horsetail is particularly difficult to eradicate, but research suggests that it absorbs weedkiller more effectively if lightly trampled before spraying.

Flowers

⚘ Shear alchemilla down to the ground to prevent plants from seeding: mounds of fresh new leaves will see you through nicely until autumn.

⚘ Cyclamen corms that have been resting can be started into growth again. Do not bring the plant inside until at least four to six flowers are in bud.

⚘ Cut out old growths of rambler roses as soon as they have finished flowering and tie in the new sappy growths, fanning out the stems as much as possible. If no new shoots have appeared, cut out one old growth entirely and prune back the side shoots on the rest.

⚘ Thin out some of the old wood on rampant honeysuckles.

⚘ Do not cut back stems of lilies after flowering. Like daffodils, lilies suck back the goodness of the stem into the bulb to build themselves up for next season.

⚘ Trim out tired flower heads of *Stachys byzantina* and of other plants such as *Geranium psilostemon*.

⚘ Cut everlastings before they come into full bloom.

⚘ Plant bulbs of forced hyacinths if you want them in flower for Christmas. A few bowls now, followed by a few next month, will give you a succession of blooms. Use bulb fibre or compost in the bowl and set the bulbs so that their noses are just above the surface of the compost. Water them well. Store the bowl in a cool place (not more than 48°F/9°C) for 8–11 weeks. Bring the bowl into the warm when the flower buds are pushing out from the bulbs. Flowering should be in full swing three weeks after the bulbs come into the light.

Vegetables

⚘ Harvest baby beet, lettuce, French beans and carrots.

⚘ Make further sowings if you need them

of mustard and cress and radish.

❦ There is still time to sneak in a last sowing of carrots which will provide fresh roots in autumn.

❦ Pick cobs of sweetcorn when the silky tassels on the ends have begun to wither. The kernels should still be soft enough for you to stick a thumbnail into them. White milky juice will ooze out.

❦ Clear away peas and beans that have finished cropping. Compost the haulms.

❦ Pull up onions and leave them to ripen on top of the ground until the green tops have withered away.

Fruit

❦ Early apples such as 'Discovery' and 'George Cave' should be picked as soon as the stems part easily from the branch.

❦ Peaches may also be ready to pick. Do not leave peaches to ripen on the tree or they may drop. A day in a warm kitchen will finish them off more safely.

❦ Cut out old fruited stems of loganberries and tie new canes in their place.

❦ Summer pruning of trained trees such as apples and pears encourages fruiting spurs. Shorten all mature side shoots to within three leaves of the base cluster of leaves. New shoots springing from existing shoots should be treated even more harshly. Cut them back to one leaf.

Propagating

❦ Take cuttings of zonal and ivy-leaved pelargoniums.

❦ Choose 3–4in/7–10cm cuttings from non-flowering shoots of lavender and stick them in a pot or a shady cold frame in sandy compost. Keep them watered.

❦ Take cuttings of *Artemisia arborescens* senecio and other grey-leaved shrubs.

❦ Cut back hard any particularly good violas and pansies that you want to increase and cover the crown of the plant with a finely sifted mixture of sandy soil. This will encourage some good new growths. You can pull these out with a few roots attached and pot them up to grow on as fresh plants.

❦ Take tip cuttings of indoor plants such as coleus, tradescantia, zebrina and busy lizzies. When rooted and growing away, pinch out the tops of the cuttings to encourage bushy growth.

❦ Take cuttings of rosemary, thyme and sage, pulling off shoots about 6in/15cm long with a good heel and lining them out 2–3in/5–7cm deep in fine, sandy soil. Firm down the soil round the cuttings and keep watered.

❦ Take cuttings of slightly tender perennials such as penstemon, felicia and argyranthemum. These will need protection through the winter.

September

Planting an Alcoholic Hedge

For taking away the backs of your knees, there is
nothing like a slug of sloe gin. We have a batch now
seething quietly in the back of a dark cupboard. It
was started last November and is getting pleasantly
close to maturity. It was a foul, cold, windy day when
we picked the fruit. It usually is, with sloes, for they
are scarcely ready before the leaves have dropped
from the trees.

In country areas, they are common in mixed
hedgerows, but there is no reason why you should
not plant them in town. They could be part of an
alcoholic hedge, a mixture of sloe and elder (for
flower champagne and berry wine), with cherry plums
to make into liqueur and filberts or Kent cobnuts to
eat with them. What can a Leyland cypress offer
compared with this fecundity? Nothing but arid,
alien evergreenness. It might as well be plastic.

The sloe or blackthorn is a member of the big plum
family. It is called *Prunus spinosa*, after the thorny
tips of the short shoots. The thorns are what makes
it such a good hedging plant. Sheep can't push
through. Nor can vandals. Left to itself, it makes a
shrubby sort of tree, rarely more than 12ft/4m high.

The wood is dark, a counterfoil to the wreaths of
white blossom that cover it in March and early April
before the leaves come out. The leaves are small and

oval. The fruit, mostly stone, is darkest purple, no bigger than a grape and with a rich pewter bloom.

You can get hold of plants from the Kingsfield Conservation Nursery, which specializes in native trees, shrubs and wild flowers, or from the Perrie Hale Forest Nursery, which keeps forest trees and hedging plants. Both do mail order.

Since blackthorns are wild plants, often growing in tough, exposed situations, they do not need cosseting in the garden. They will need drashing from time to time, more to restrict their girth than their height. The thickest and best hedges are those that are laid, but this is a farmer's skill, rarely a gardener's. You need to lurk around ploughing matches and other such agricultural meets where hedging competitions are often held. Then it is a matter of bribing the winner to come and look at your patch.

It will be some time, though, before you need to worry about this little manoeuvre. Blackthorns are best established when they are about 12–18in/30–45cm high, and though they quickly make a hedgy-looking mass, you can snip them whenever you want, to stop them straying over paths or other shrubs. Set the plants about 15in/38cm apart. To get through the labour of planting, best done in October and November, think of the gin.

To make this, you need between 12–16oz/about 400g sloes, some sugar (3–6oz/80–160g) and a bottle of gin, duty free if possible, because then you won't fret about it being a waste. You also need an empty wide-mouth jar with a screw-on lid.

Prick the sloes with a fork and pack them into the jar with a sprinkling of sugar between each layer. When the bottle is full, top it up with gin and screw down the lid. Leave the mixture in a dark place until the evenings of the next season are cold enough to warrant taking it out of its hiding place. Strain off the liquid into a clean bottle. It is a very good thing to take on winter picnics. Standing up, you are aware what it is doing to you. Sitting down, it is lethal.

The most interesting and useful hedges are mixed ones – good for birds as well as us. Elder grows so easily it is practically a weed, but if you coppice it regularly, pruning out some of the oldest growths each year on a three-year rotation, it can be kept within bounds. It does not mesh in the same way as blackthorn, so on its own, unlaid, it won't keep animals in or people out. It grows very fast, though, and provides a good tall summer screen. And two sources of alcohol.

From the flower heads – wide, flat, creamy heads of blossom which appear in June – you can make champagne. Our middle daughter, who had the misfortune to be born during one of our more penniless periods, was christened in elderflower champagne. The timing of the christening is crucial. This stuff has an uncertain cellar life: it tends to explode.

Making it is simple, compared with the problems of cellaring. Put four or six heads of elderflower in a plastic bucket with the juice and the thinly pared rind of a lemon, 1½lb/700g sugar and two tablespoons of white wine vinegar. Cover the lot with a gallon of cold water and let it steep for 24 hours before straining the liquid into bottles. You will soon see bubbles building up inside the bottles. It is then rather a matter of luck whether the bottle is man enough to contain the brew. Six weeks is about the right time for drinking. If you can get it through a year you can call it vintage.

As an ingredient of a hedge, the cheapest elder is the wild one, *Sambucus nigra*, with green leaves and creamy heads of blossom. It grows to about the same height as the blackthorn, but much faster. Sappy new shoots can make 5ft/1.5m in a season. It is very easy from cuttings, taken in November. You need lengths of hardwood about 12–15in/30–38cm long. Stick them in a row in a nursery bed and transplant them to the hedge after a year.

For fitness of purpose there is nothing to beat common elder, but if you want something more gardenesque, you can choose 'Aurea', a form with golden foliage. It becomes green as the summer wears on. 'Aureomarginata' has leaves with yellow margins. The problem with these in a drunken hedge is that

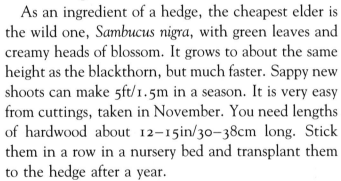

SEPTEMBER

the best leaves come from cutting the elder hard back each winter. This will be at the expense of the flowers, so you won't get your champagne.

The form called *laciniata* does not need such drastic treatment. It has leaves so finely cut, they look like ferns, but it is not as vigorous as the wild kind. There are other forms too, with purple leaves, white speckled leaves and some with pink flowers rather than cream. The national collection is held at the National Trust's garden at Wallington in Northumberland.

Berries are mostly reddish black, though there is a rather pointless form, 'Viridis', with green berries and one for the aesthetes, 'Alba', with white berries. I am not sure what sort of wine these would make.

Having sashayed your way through the summer on elderflower champagne, the berries, which come in September, provide a second excuse for a binge. There are always far more than you need, but the birds will be grateful for the leftovers and will then customize your car for you with surreal splodges of purplish-grey.

Wine making is a more complicated business than the gin or champagne recipes. You need demijohns and airlocks or, in the quantities Mrs Beeton suggests, a wooden cask. Get a book from the library and experiment. The best type is one that is made from 2lb/1 kilo elderberries, 8oz/250g raisins, 3lb/

1.5 kilo demerara sugar, ¼oz/5g cloves, a cinnamon stick, ½oz/10g root ginger, a lemon and 8pt/4.5 litres water. It is very good mulled.

Elders are even less bother than blackthorns and will grow well in shade. The bark is pale, furrowed and corky, the new shoots pithy rather than woody. The bruised leaves have an unpleasant, sour smell. Elders like damp soil better than dry and, like anything you plant, will do better with an annual mulch of compost than without.

The cherry plum has fruits twice the size of sloes and half as bitter. It is called *Prunus cerasifera*. It is more tree-like than the sloe, often growing taller, though you can trim it to size. Both trees, left to their own devices, become as wide as they are high. The cherry plum blossoms in February and March – white flowers, slightly larger than the sloe's. The fruit ripens in late summer.

It makes an excellent hedge or screen and, mixed with sloe, gives a long season of spring blossom. Nursery plants are likely to be 18–24in/45–60cm high and you should set them about 2ft/60cm apart. The hedge can be pruned back at any time of the year. The fruits are too fiddly for pies, but make a good liqueur or wine, becoming more like port the longer you keep it.

Once the hedge is reasonably established, say to about 4ft/1.2m, you could add to its alcoholic potential by planting cultivated blackberries at intervals along it and training the shoots along the hedge, tying them in roughly where needed. Blackberries call for the same sort of treatment as raspberries. Each year, after you have gathered the fruit, you must cut out the old growths on which the fruit was borne and tie in the new ones that spring like a fountain from the base. Cultivated varieties provide fruit that is larger, earlier and less pippy than wild blackberries. Try 'Bedford Giant' or 'Loch Ness'.

A London Garden

Do actors make good garden designers? Discuss, taking in on the way ex-actor Anthony Noel's back yard at 17 Fulham Park Gardens, London. On the whole, the answer is probably 'Yes'. Actors understand the art of illusion, of creating moods, which is an important part of garden making. They use props well and are not scared of grand gestures which the rest of us might fear we could not bring off.

Anthony Noel's grand gesture is a monumental urn mounted on a plinth in the back left-hand corner of his garden. It had arrived only in the morning of the day that I visited, but was already perfectly in place, washed over with instant ageing liquid and with greenery arranged round its feet.

There was much discussion about how the urn should be dressed. Should it be left empty, or should it perhaps have in it the large silver-leaved astelia presently flourishing in another, smaller urn in the corresponding corner of the garden close to the house? A glaucous-leaved rose, *R. glauca*, is growing conveniently close to the new urn. Should some tendrils of this be wrapped round the plinth, or would a specially planted clematis do a better clothing job?

The garden is only 40ft/12m long by 17ft/5.2m wide, so the introduction of the 6ft/1.8m urn has been a bold move. Anthony Noel was enchanted by it. It had been an object of desire since he first saw it, or rather its twin, on a job he was doing in Scotland. Acting now takes a back seat to his career in garden design ('I wish it had happened years ago') and he had been planting up the same urns in a hotel conservatory in Ayrshire.

It joins a gallimaufry of architectural objects in the garden: stone balls balanced round the boundary walls, pineapple finials decorating the tops of two pillars of ivy, a shallow urn in the back right-hand corner of the plot, with a dumpy pyramid of clipped box in the middle, surrounded by carefully manicured plants of a neat white-flowered marguerite.

In the brick paved passage that leads from kitchen door to garden are huge terracotta pots swagged and decorated. Two carefully clipped box balls are the centrepieces of these tubs, surrounded by a froth of petunias. The trick, he says, is to shear them down in late July when they start to get leggy and difficult and then to feed them liberally with fast-acting foliar feed. There is a good deal of clipped box, a carefully trained spiral by the seat against the left-hand wall, a small neat hedge around the raised bed that stretches along two-thirds of the back boundary where the new urn now stands.

The best box act is a series of clipped balls, each in a terracotta pot, arranged in two rows along the middle of the right-hand wall, with a trough of pebbles behind. It is extremely mannered, but in keeping with the rest of the garden, which is a very conscious creation. There is a pleasant dottiness about this assemblage of topiary spheres, mirroring the rows of stone balls on the wall above, that saves it from pretentiousness.

The colours throughout are muted. Foliage is more important than flowers – evergreen, silver and vari-egated, with a curtain of golden hops flung over the right-hand boundary wall. Variegated ivy is the most dominant feature against the back wall, with white wisteria and white-flowered jasmine trained against the house wall. The fat fleshy leaves of London pride are trimmed to make a border round the raised bed, and grey-leaved helichrysum wanders around at will in the bed by the right-hand wall, covering gaps where earlier there were columbines and violas and chequered snakeshead fritillaries.

White and purple are the dominant flower colours – in late summer, the whites of the annual petunias and the daisy-flowered Danish marguerites. Stray purple blooms are left over from clematis such as *C. viticella* 'Purpurea Plena Elegans', 'Etoile Violette' and 'Royal Velours'. When the large-leaved hostas start to fall apart in the back right-hand corner, mauve autumn crocus and small *Cyclamen hederifolium* bob up to take their place.

The design is simple: a rectangle of lawn, surrounded by paving, in turn edged by borders which run up to the walls. The textures are good: immaculate turf ('I'm a terrible old fusspot'), edged to fit the ins and outs of the York stone around it. This is one of the details I liked most about the garden. Cut with dead straight parallel edges, the grass would not have been so effective.

In many London gardens, grass is a disaster, for the smaller the patch, the better kept it has to be. In this garden, where every leaf and petal is tweaked and manipulated to best effect, it provides a soft, cool centre for the overall scheme. Anthony Noel calls it a romantic garden, but it is perhaps too deliberate, too calculated in its effects to be romantic. It is vogueish, stylish, not a garden to walk into with the wrong socks on. But visitors – however clad – are

SEPTEMBER

welcome when the garden is open under the National Gardens Scheme.

In the sunny bed against the house wall is a collection of Mediterranean plants, mostly grey and silver, queened over by the astelia in its urn. There is a group of furry-leaved *Salvia argentea*, dissuaded firmly from flowering by the simple expedient of nipping out the flowering shoots. The leaves are the plants' chief glory, but quickly go to pot once the plant starts to flower.

At the back of the bed is sea-green melianthus, the most handsome foliage plant of all and, in this London patch, more reliably hardy than it would be in exposed northern gardens. Rosemary, mottled silybum, artemisia and the small-leaved helichrysum fill in between, thriving in ground that has been well-dressed with grit to improve drainage. As many Mediterranean plants die in this country from damp as they do from cold. Grit keeps their necks dry.

In the right-hand border are groups of black and white plants. The dark, almost black, grass-like ophiopogon weaves through silver-leaved helichrysum. White-flowered hostas and the fine Japanese anemone 'Honorine Jobert' contrast with the velvety black-faced viola 'Molly Sanderson'.

Some of the best plantings are in the quietest and least propitious places. The edging of London pride and box round the edge of the raised bed is lifted

immeasurably by clumps of a silver painted Japanese
fern, tucked in along the foot of a low retaining wall.
The passage outside the kitchen door, often wasted
space, has in it some of the best combinations in the
garden – fat, waxy aeoniums, a crested hart's tongue
fern, various sempervivums, the snaky small spurge
Euphorbia myrsinites. Here there is shade for much of
the day and plants can find a cool root run under the
brick paving.

Now that the garden is so comprehensively 'done',
Anthony Noel is turning his attention to the
kitchen, the approach to the garden. He sees it as a
rusticated grotto, the walls *trompe-l'oeiled* with tro-
phies and shields. I am worrying what he is going to
do about the cooker.

A Flower of Manhood

I feel that, like George Eliot, I should adopt a pseudonym to write this piece about dahlias. Dahlia growing is a male preserve, as you will discover if you lurk around the edges of any show, such as the National Dahlia Show, held in London in late summer. I have eavesdropped on a hundred esoteric male conversations on these occasions, trying to find an answer to the conundrum, but it eludes me.

Proponents of the power theory would say that it is the sheer bulk that attracts: massive, meaty tubers, huge fleshy leaves, stalks like drainpipes. But this is too simple an explanation. There are plenty of growers, particularly in the south-west, whose passion is the pompons – tight-lipped little flowers, round and hard as a piece of porcelain, no more than 2in/5cm across, balanced perfectly on long, thin stems. I have seen veterans handling blooms of 'Hallmark', a deep lavender-pink pompon of symmetrical perfection, as though they were touching the cheek of an angel.

There are plenty, of course, who loathe dahlias. They usually know very little about them, but are conditioned to give a little shudder, to wince sensitively, if the word comes up in polite conversation. In these circumstances, the best thing is to say, 'Oh, but Gertrude Jekyll *loved* them,' which that renowned gardener and plantswoman did.

Because they have such a high profile as exhibition flowers, dahlias are surrounded with a great deal of mumbo-jumbo. They are actually extremely willing plants, not difficult to grow adequately; adequately enough, that is, to please you in the garden even if not to meet the stricter requirements of judges at the show bench. The large varieties are not easy to use in mixed plantings. They come into bloom late, usually not before mid-August, and need plenty of elbow room while they are growing. They could, however, be combined with perennials such as oriental poppies, whose season is very early. The poppy foliage can be sheared away when it has finished flowering and the dahlia plants will swell to fill the gap.

At Overbecks, a National Trust garden in Devon, smaller varieties are brilliantly used in hot colour combinations: 'Bishop of Llandaff', bronze-purple foliage with brilliant red flowers, with *Salvia fulgens*; another dark-leaf dahlia, 'David Howard', with *Argyranthemum* 'Vancouver', or with crocosmia and yellow coreopsis. Tony Murdoch, the gardener there, also uses the bedding dahlia 'Redskin', which grows about 15in/38cm high and has dark foliage and flowers of scarlet, crimson and orange, in a mixed planting with mottled silybum, canna and the phormium 'Sundowner'. 'Redskin' is grown from seed, started off early in a heated greenhouse and set out at the end of May, when one hopes that frost is as

SEPTEMBER

distant a memory as chilblains. Frost is anathema to dahlias. They shrivel up at the first touch of it and it is a pathetic sight. In a mild winter they may bloom until Christmas. We had a red dahlia on the Christmas pudding one year as the birds had eaten all the holly berries.

Raising them from seed is not the usual way to get hold of dahlias. It is more likely that you will buy tubers, or cuttings, or well-grown plants. Tubers are sent out by specialist growers between November and March. Plants raised from cuttings are dispatched between late April and June. Ken Aplin, a postman who grows superb dahlias – more than 300 of them – in his allotment by the River Frome, says that good stock is vital. Nothing worthy will ever come from a wizened, prepackaged tuber that has been hanging round longer than it ought in a garden centre, he says firmly. If you go for rooted plants, these can go straight in the ground at the end of May (a couple of weeks later in the north).

They need good ground, a position where they will get sun for at least half the day. Mr Aplin rotavates plenty of muck into his ground before top-dressing with Vitax Q4. He does no extra feeding, but plenty of watering. At the rate they grow, dahlias lap up water faster than dehydrated dingoes.

Staking is vital. There is a lot of wind resistance in a dahlia dressed overall. Three canes and plenty of soft twine in the usual answer. Through June and most of July, all you will have to do is watch them grow. Then comes the fiddly bit: disbudding. For show dahlias this is essential, but a little population control is good for garden plants as well. Without your intervention, too many flowers will be produced and the bush will become a muddle.

On most growths, there is a boss bud and two lesser outriders. Although it runs counter to all one's natural sympathy for the underdog, the subsidiary buds, rather like the sideshoots of tomatoes, must be nipped out before they get too big. The remaining bud will then have unlimited resources to develop into a fine long-stemmed bloom.

Mr Aplin, who is astonishingly low-tech for a showman, does not spray his plants, but if there is a bad plague of greenfly, it might be necessary. Earwigs are his only enemies and he deals with them by squirting a few drops of paraffin down inside each of the hollow canes he uses as stakes. Earwigs rest in the canes after nocturnal forays.

The giant decoratives are the dahlias that hypnotize me, like a rabbit in front of a blazing headlamp. They are not the easiest varieties to keep on their feet. Some grow more than 5ft/1.5m high and need not so much staking as buttressing. But who, having seen 'Trelawny' in fighting form – whirling wheels of bronze, almost 12in/30cm across – could fail to be

SEPTEMBER

205

transfixed? Who could pass by the sumptuous magenta-purple globes of 'Night Editor' without a second glance?

Mr Aplin could. He is not a giant decorative man, although he allows the clear yellow 'Alva's Supreme' into his select allotment group. He is, as he puts it, 'more of a pompon and ball man'. In this instance the balls come either miniature (2–4in/5–10cm) or small (4–6in/10–15cm). His champion this year is 'Kathryn's Cupid', a miniature ball of slightly salmon pink. 'It'll be a pleasure to cut those,' he said. The purple 'Risca Miner' is his favourite small ball.

As for the cactus-flowered varieties, with petals rolled round like quills, he would recommend the pink 'Athalie'. I would add the deep red 'Doris Day'. Among the small decoratives, he likes the yellow 'Ruskin Diane'. Being a showman, he goes for form before anything else, a good depth of flower in the decoratives, and a perfect arrangement of petals. I go first for colour, which is what puts me off the sulphurous yellow of so many show flowers such as the cactus-flowered 'Klankstad Kerkrade'.

If you get bitten by the dahlia bug, you will, after the drunken delight of watching them bloom in their first season, have to face the problem of what to do with them through the winter. Being in a favoured patch of England, we leave ours in the ground and 70 per cent survive even in the tough winters. Standard practice is to lift them when they have been stopped by frost, cut down the stems to an inch, dry the tubers out carefully and store them in a cool, frost-free place until planting time in May. Experts bore down right through the stump of the main stem with a screw-driver to aerate the roots.

⚘

THE POTAGER: PART ONE
HERE'S HOW YOUR GARDEN GROWS

Potager, like bidet and treillage, is a word that hovers uneasily on the outskirts of English. It still feels too Frenchified to use without feeling self-conscious. Hors-d'oeuvre, already bandied about by Pope and Smollett in the middle of the eighteenth century, trips off the tongue without trouble, perhaps because there is no precise equivalent in English to replace it. For the same reason we will have to get our tongues round potager.

Used the English way, it means posh veg, grown as part of a formal design, mixed up with flowers and fruit and whatever else makes them look decorative as well as useful. In cottage gardens, flowers and veg-etables have been growing together for centuries, mostly by accident. The potager replaces randomness with order.

Villandry, the great Renaissance château west of

1

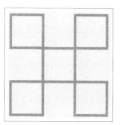

2

3

Tours in France, has the world's most famous potager – acres of it, divided into nine equal squares, each containing a different design of formal beds edged in box. The plot I have in mind is about 16ft/5m square.

This is the first in a series which, at monthly intervals, will show how to potager such a plot. You have the winter months to design and construct the framework and to order the necessary plants and seeds for take-off next spring. Would-be vegetable growers can now have your carrots as well as your violas.

Some starting points for a design are shown here. Anyone prone to doodling in the margin of their newspaper while waiting for a Northern Line train will find this bit easy. The main danger lies in overcomplication. Some central vortex is useful in pulling the whole design together. It also gives you the chance to use a gazebo, trellis or other structure to give height, a focal point, at the centre.

A square lends itself more easily than a rectangle to symmetry in design. The smaller the garden, the more symmetry becomes it. The 16ft/5m square, depending on how you divide it up, will give you between eight and ten separate compartments for planting. Not all the paths need be of the same width or importance.

While the wet days over the next month can be pleasantly filled with drafting alternative layouts, the dry days call for more physical effort. Preparation of the soil is vital. This is where you can sense readers turning away in droves from the whole idea of the potager. Interior decorating has just that effect on me. All the instructions about preparing walls before you paper is music to DIY ears, but discouraging to anyone more interested in the effect than the under-pinning. Soil is different, though. It is not inert, like plaster and Polyfilla. It is a vital, living medium, to be treated with consideration and respect. It is not inexhaustible. It gets as tired and hungry and ill as we do. By treating it only with doses of chemicals, you turn it into a kind of drug addict, able to function only with stronger and stronger doses of junk.

In natural habitats, soil is replenished with a litter of dying vegetation and animal droppings, gradually pulled down into the earth by worms and insects. The garden is an unnatural habitat, dying vegetation whisked away like dirty coffee mugs from the sitting room. In a small garden, you may be loath to give space to a compost bin. If so, compensate by blanketing your plot with some bought compost. Anything bulky and organic will do: mushroom compost, spent hops, whatever is on offer at the garden centre.

In town gardens where there is often no access from front to back except through the house, this is easier said than done. The effort will be repaid a thousandfold. And you will be buoyed up by the

4

5

SEPTEMBER

virtuous feeling of having Done the Right Thing.

The patch itself needs to be chosen with care. It can be part shaded, but not overhung. It also needs to be level. The outline designs on the previous page show several different options. You can incorporate a small paved area at the centre (No. 3) for a large pot or a small table and chairs. You can make some paths wide enough (No. 5) to take an overhead arbour of ironwork or trellis and cover them with runner beans or outdoor cucumbers wound round with clematis. Consider all the features you want to fit in before you fix on the design.

Before you start to lay out the design on the ground, the whole patch must be forked over, hefty weeds such as dandelion and dock removed, and the earth raked to leave a smoothish, levelish square. The larding with compost can wait until you have marked out the beds. You do not want to waste good compost on paths.

Mark out the design with sticks and lengths of string. This will lead you inexorably on to the question of paths and edgings. The answers will be dictated by taste and cost. You can, of course, leave the paths as trodden earth. The design will be muted this way, lacking contrasts of colour and texture between paths and vegetable beds. They will also be muddy after rain. The advantage of trodden earth paths is that they cost nothing. And they are easily re-routed, if you feel like a change in layout.

One of the cheapest treatments is to cover the paths with chipped or ground bark. Lay it over black polythene if you want to cut down on weeding, not if (as I do) you like the idea of the bark itself slowly transmuting to soil. Ground, composted bark disappears faster, but gives a smooth, sleek finish. Chipped bark is coarse and rustic in effect. Both are dark, treacle-coloured.

If you use bark, which kicks about easily, you will probably need an edging to the beds, to prevent the one straying into the other. Lengths of board are simple to fix with a few wooden pegs bashed into the ground to keep them where you want them. Avoid the corrugated plastic edging which is sold in rolls. It draws attention to itself without having the looks to warrant it.

If you use a more permanent form of paving for the paths, you can dispense with fixed edgings, relying on borders of parsley, alpine strawberries and the like to keep the earth vaguely in place. There will always be some sweeping up to do. Birds don't understand the pleasures of clean paths. Blackbirds have beaks that excavate like JCBs.

You can also still buy old-fashioned edging tiles in various patterns. Terracotta rope edge tiles, each 7in/ 18cm high and 9in/23cm long, are the most common and Agriframes sell new ones in packs. Salvage firms

SEPTEMBER

usually have edging tiles in stock, too. Conservation Building Products Ltd offers a wide variety of different designs.

Old bricks make good paths. DIY experts will suck their teeth knowingly if you use indoor bricks outside. Yes, they do flake in bad frosts, but they do not disintegrate entirely and the texture and colour of ordinary bricks is infinitely more pleasant than the unvarying liverish look of what they call engineering brick. Stableyard bricks are equally good, shallower and cross-hatched on the top in a regular diamond pattern.

Jobs for the Month

General

* Repair damaged lawn edges by cutting a rectangle of turf behind the edge and then re-laying it round the reverse way so that the worn edge is on the inside. Sift a little earth over the join.

* Spike over established lawns to aerate them and top-dress them with a mixture of compost and sand.

* Rooted sections of chives, mint and marjoram can be gently levered away from clumps in the ground and set in pots of compost for a winter supply of fresh herbs.

* Clip virginia creeper back from windows and haul it out of gutters.

* Mulch wherever you can with whatever bulky material you can get hold of. Mushroom compost is excellent. So is home-made compost and grass cuttings with fallen leaves mixed with them.

Flowers

* Annuals such as poppies, calendula, larkspur, limnanthes, love-in-a-mist, clarkia and cornflower will make an early show next year if they are sown outside now where you want them to flower. Protect them with netting against marauding cats and birds. Leave any

necessary thinning until next spring.

* Continue to plant prepared hyacinths for indoor flowering; 15 September is the last possible day for planting if you want them out for Christmas.

* Tulips also make good potted plants, but must have at least 12 weeks buried or kept in a cool, dark place before they are brought into the warm.

* Start planting daffodil bulbs, which always look better in large groups. If planting in grass, choose a spot where their dying leaves and the lengthening grass will not irritate you to the extent that you mow too soon.

* Cut off and dry seed heads from leeks, alliums, Chinese lanterns, honesty and opium poppies and hang them upside down to dry for winter decoration.

* Houseplants need less food and water as growth slows down for winter.

* Start to clear out summer bedding plants to make way for autumn plantings of wallflowers, sweet Williams and tulips. Choose wallflowers with the growing tips pinched out to make compact, bushy plants.

* Mildew often affects Michaelmas daisies at this time of year. The spores overwinter on stems and leaves. Cut out all diseased stems after flowering and burn them. Control mildew by using a sys-

temic fungicide. Start spraying in the spring and continue at fortnightly intervals. Old *novi-belgii* types are particularly prone. Replace them instead with *Aster × frikartii*.

⚘ Biennials and perennials grown from seed can be planted out in their permanent positions.

⚘ Clear rotting leaves of iris and water lilies from garden ponds.

⚘ Houseplants that have been standing out for the summer should start to come indoors again. Remove dead and damaged leaves, check staking and watch for pests such as whitefly which multiply in the more encouraging indoor climate.

⚘ For a spring display, sow seed of a hardy pansy. Scatter seed thinly in trays of compost, cover with more moist compost and wrap the tray in clear polythene covered with newspaper. Remove the covers when the seeds have germinated (usually about a week). After about three weeks, prick seedlings out separately into small pots. Plant out in late February or March.

⚘ Put colchicum bulbs to flower inside on saucers of small pebbles. Keep the bulbs well watered, but not drowned. Within a few weeks they will show their long-necked, crocus-like flowers.

⚘ Clean out ragged old flower heads of climbing hydrangea, making the cut where the stem joins the main branch.

Vegetables

⚘ Plant Japanese onions now for an early crop next summer. They fill the gap before other onions come on stream.

⚘ Spinach can be sown now to overwinter and give an early crop in April next year.

⚘ Lift potatoes and store them away from the light.

⚘ Clear runner beans and French beans from the vegetable plot.

Fruit

⚘ After picking the last of the peaches and nectarines, wall-trained trees will need pruning and the new shoots tying in to replace the old fruited shoots. Cut out entirely any shoots that grow straight out of the front of the tree at right angles.

⚘ Morello cherries fruit on growth made the previous year, not on older wood. Dissuade them from fruiting only on the outer fringes by cutting away one or two older branches now, to a point where a strong new shoot has broken out.

OCTOBER

Spring in Autumn

One of the best things about being a gardening corre-
spondent is the cast-iron excuse that it gives me to
abandon washing up, shopping and other hideous
duties and go gardening instead. The rich warm still
days of the first half of October can provide the best
conditions of the whole year. The soil is reasonably
moist after the September rain, but not so wet that
it cannot be worked easily. The ground is still warm
and the air too, so that dahlias are bursting with new
blooms and penstemons have as much flower on them
as at any time during the summer.

There is an element of lottery about these gorgeous
days of October. Each one, you feel, might be the
last. Nothing can be taken for granted. This might
be the last day you see the salvias in bloom. This
might be the last chance to clap your nose to one of
the long scented trumpets of the white tobacco
flower, *Nicotiana sylvestris*.

There have been decisions to make. I had to find a
home for half a dozen bulbs of *Nectaroscordum siculum
bulgaricum* sent to me by a friend. It is one of the
plants that taxonomists have been playing catch
with. First it was an allium, *A. siculum*; then they
decided it was a different allium, *A. bulgaricum*. Now
it is unpronounceable. The stems shoot up to more
than 3ft/90cm. Each has a topknot of dangling

flowers, cream flushed with maroon and green. As the flowers die they turn themselves upright, the seed heads making small cones on the stems. The leaves stink. E.A. Bowles, the Edwardian gardener, said that he had difficulty in deciding whether the smell 'most resembles an escape of gas or a new mackintosh'.

After wandering round the garden with the bag of bulbs, mentally drawing smelly 3ft/90cm stems in among existing groups of plants, I finally settled for a newly cleared patch, a quarter-circle made between two arms of the house. A newish abutilon stands in the corner where the house walls meet, with a 'Wedding Day' rose and *Solanum jasminoides* flourishing now with pale clusters of flowers on the south-facing part of the wall.

The bulbs, which bloom in late spring, finally went in front of and around two other plants, which I recently acquired and which have been waiting for a home. The first is a herbaceous phlomis, *P. tuberosa* 'Amazone', a bushy-looking plant from Siberia, with spikes of lilac sage-like, lipped flowers arranged at intervals up the stem. The leaves look coarse, but I have a weakness for phlomis. Once you become intrigued by a particular family of plants, you start excusing their faults.

The second is an echinacea. 'White Swan' was the first of this family to find a place in the garden. Fresh flowers are still coming up. At first there is a large prickly-looking centre disc surrounded by greenish-white ray petals. As the flower matures, the disc pushes up into a cone and changes colour from green to a deep tawny yellow. The petals then hang down like a fringe round the cone. When the petals finally drop, the cones turn chestnut brown. At this stage they are useful for drying.

The new echinacea, E. purpurea, has the same central boss, but with mauve-crimson flowers and dark-flushed foliage. It grows to about 4ft/1.2m and does not need staking. That is a bonus. I am a lazy staker and try to put plants close enough together to prop each other up, like drunks at a bus stop. It works as long as the weather is kind. Gales and rain bring the whole lot crashing down.

The friend who sent the bulbs suggested magenta Gladiolus byzantinus and lime-green Euphorbia palustris as companions. I like the idea. Unfortunately I haven't got clumps of either that I can spare at the moment, so I will have to wait before adding those to the group.

The general perception of the October garden is of gold and yellow and red and brown, a kilim carpet laid on the earth. In fact there is a great deal of purple and blue around, with the salvias shining out most brightly of all. The newest addition this year is Salvia guaranitica, which used to be S. ambigens. (Why do the easy names always change to impossible ones?)

'To see this plant in full flower in October is to taste of the fullness of gardening,' writes Graham Stuart Thomas in *Perennial Garden Plants*. A new edition of this masterpiece was published in 1990 and is invaluable. Alongside the descriptions of plants, in alphabetical order, you get suggestions for companion planting.

For *S. guaranitica* Mr Thomas suggests the tall yellow *Hypericum* 'Rowallane'. Mine is in different company, behind a mound of the monster catmint 'Six Hills Giant', still going strong, and next to a variegated aralia, just beginning to drop its leaves.

The salvia is a tall, rangy grower, up to 5ft/1.5m, and comes from Brazil. It has brilliantly blue flowers which yawn like the pictures of hippopotamuses you see on wild life programmes. It is not reliably hardy, but I am willing to gamble on its survival. North of the Wash, the odds would drop dramatically.

Less intense blue, more sky-coloured, is *Salvia uliginosa*. Its name suggests it likes bogs, but it does not seem to suffer in a dry summer. Whereas the upper and lower jaws of *S. guaranitica*'s flowers are equally matched, *S. uliginosa* has a splayed-out bottom lip, shaped like a tiny pansy, and a mere remnant of a top lip, whitish rather than blue. Each individual flower is tiny, but they mass together at the end of graceful 5ft/1.5m stems.

OCTOBER

On its own it would probably need support. It looks too ethereal to look after itself properly. I have it surrounded by a stockade of purple-flowered *Verbena bonariensis* (now *V. patagonica*), equally tall and thin, but with wiry stems that are strong enough to support a few passengers. All three plants are South American.

The verbena has overwintered happily for the last two winters. It also self-seeds copiously. The first year, I left the plants untouched after their wintering, but they got impossibly enormous and messy. This spring I cut them to the ground. Fresh new growth sprang up and has been much more manageable. Some has seeded into a bush of the *alba* rose 'Céleste' and earlier, in June, the flowers of both were out together.

Although there are several soft blues about – caryopteris, with foliage smelling of balsam, and late ceanothus – the only other plant that can match the salvias for intensity of colour is *Ceratostigma willmottianum*. It is an open, floppy sort of shrub, rather lacking bulk, but you can cheat and plant three close together. The flowers appear in clusters at the end of the stems. A cluster during its life might produce thirty or more flowers, but no more than three or four will be out at the same time. It is enough. Any more and the retina would start peeling away from the eyeball.

A Perfect Pear Tree

It is harder to bring a pear to luscious perfection than it is an apple. The difficulty lies off rather than on the tree. A pear changes more radically than an apple after it has been picked. It does not ripen on the tree. Its flesh, still hard when the fruit is gathered, gradually softens in storage until it has the melting texture of butter.

The point of no return is quickly reached. The biggest disappointment of a pear fancier's life is, after smelling, stroking and admiring the colour of a seemingly perfect fruit, to sink his teeth into the flesh and meet a grey, runny, slightly alcoholic mess just under the skin. Pears are like Russian statesmen: the outside appearance gives little indication of what is going on under the surface.

The problem of storing pears at the correct temperature and bringing them to table in exactly the right state may be one of the reasons why they are not so widely grown as they were. Dessert pears were once a benchmark of a head gardener's expertise: 'Citron des Carmes' and 'Jargonelle' for the beginning of the season, 'Joséphine de Malines' and 'Beurré Rance' for the end.

In the nineteenth century, the Royal Horticultural Society had 622 varieties of pear growing in its gardens at Chiswick. There are still seventy different

kinds available from specialist nurseries and nearly
500 sorts maintained in the National Fruit Collection
at Brogdale in Kent.

Pears were never British natives. Their natural
home is in the warm countries round the Mediterranean. You need to bear this in mind when you are
thinking of planting them in the garden for they need
more warmth and sunshine than apples to fruit well.
Choose a sheltered spot that does not get hit by frost.
Pears generally flower two weeks earlier than apples,
so the blossom is more prone to frost damage. In
exposed gardens, they need a sheltering windbreak.

The trees are tolerant of a reasonably wide range
of soils, though they will struggle and sulk in areas of
shallow chalk. Light sandy soils need bulking up with
masses of muck or other humus. Carting muck is an
unglamorous task, but a pear is a long-lived tree and,
if well-grown, a beautiful one. Time spent improving
its home will envelop you in a tangible glow of self-
righteousness; the pear will benefit as well.

The wild pear, *Pyrus communis*, is a deep-rooted,
slow-maturing tree, able to make the best of soils that
are unsuitable for other fruit. Most pear trees that
you buy, apart from some half-standards, will have
been grafted on to quince rootstock which restricts
the overall size of the tree and brings it into fruit
more quickly.

Quince rootstock is not so tolerant of poor soil as

the wild pear, however. It is shallower rooting and needs good soil with plenty of food and drink and not too much lime. If kept on short rations, trees on quince stock are quicker to show the effects: growth slows down, blossom does not set well and fruit does not mature. Starved pears tend to split.

Site and style of tree are questions that need to be considered hand in hand. Some of the most aristo-cratic dessert pears – 'Marie-Louise', 'Winter Nelis', 'Glou Morceau' – will do better with a wall to develop full flavour. This means growing the trees as espaliers or fans. Others, like 'Conference' and my particular favourite 'Beurré Hardy', are not so fussy and can be grown as bushes or half-standards.

Pear trees naturally have a more svelte outline than blowzy apples. They are generally upright in growth, sometimes slightly weeping. Although the present fashion is for dwarf trees, I prefer half-standards, where there is room to accommodate them. There is a certain amount of wobbling on ladders during pick-ing and pruning, but the trees, let off the dwarfing leash, develop into creatures of great elegance.

A half-standard tree will live longer than a bush, perhaps a hundred years. You can plant one knowing that when you die you will have left behind at least one thing that is a plus rather than a minus. They are ornamental as well as useful, as glorious in spring blossom as a Japanese cherry.

OCTOBER

Fruiting will depend not only on situation, but also on the amount of pimping you are prepared to engage in to arrange a decent sex life for your pear tree. 'Conference' can sort out its own, but will bear more heavily with some help from a neighbouring pear.

The varieties can be sorted into three different pollinating groups, depending on time of flowering. For the best chances of cross-pollination you should choose pears from the same group, though there is usually enough overlap between the flowering seasons to pair off trees from adjoining groups.

'Marguerite Marillat', which has enormous golden fruit, flushed with scarlet, is a neat upright tree, very suitable for small gardens. The pears are ready for eating during September and October. It flowers early and so a good companion for it might be 'Louise Bonne of Jersey', which comes into blossom at the same time. This old variety has long greenish-yellow fruit and makes a hardy, vigorous tree going up to 15ft/5m. The fruit ripens during late October and November.

One of the best pears for flavour is 'Doyenné du Comice', with huge golden fruit ready for picking in mid-October and for eating up until Christmas. As with the 'Cox' apple, however, I prefer somebody else to take on the problems of growing it, leaving me to home in, fruit-bat-style, when the thing is ready for eating. 'Comice' demands the best of con-

ditions and even when it has them is horribly susceptible to scab.

I am thinking about a pear tree to replace an
ancient apple that keeled over in a violent storm a
few months ago. For nostalgia's sake (and for its
taste), I am tempted by 'Jargonelle', an ancient pear,
old even when John Parkinson wrote of it in 1629.
'An early peare,' he said, 'somewhat long and of a
very pleasant taste.' The season is short but the fruit
is ready in August. It crops freely when it is established, is resistant to scab and is very hardy, a good
variety to try in the north. A disadvantage for some
(though not for me, as I have other pears around) is
that it needs two pollinators.

The other contestant for the apple's place is
'Joséphine de Malines', raised in 1830 at Malines in
Belgium by a veteran of Napoleon's army and named
after his wife. It has small green fruit, yellowing to a
melting, deliciously perfumed mouthful late in the
season. It is a good cropper, but the tree is only
moderately vigorous and it needs more warmth than
'Jargonelle' to develop its flavour.

Bullfinches are not too much of a problem in my
garden, but they can be murder on the buds of pear
blossom. For some reason, perhaps because the buds
fit the cut of the bullfinch's beak, 'Conference', 'Williams' and 'Merton Pride' are particularly susceptible.
'Comice' and 'Beurré Hardy' are usually left alone.

OCTOBER

Requiem for a Toolshed

This is a requiem for a toolshed – my toolshed. It was not a very grand affair – a stone lean-to, built against the east wall of the house, no more than 5 × 4ft/1.5 × 1.2m inside and just tall enough at its good end to walk into without wiping the top off your head on the lintel. It was actually built as a privy, and when we arrived here in 1974, a thunderbox was still *in situ*, quite an elaborate affair in dark stained wood, throne-like in its dimensions, with a zinc cistern built into the high wooden back.

For several years after the thunderbox had been removed from its shelter, it stood high and dry in the courtyard by the stables. The children became excessively fond of it, and all visitors were led up to it, as to a shrine, and invited to try it for size.

We still have it, although it is no longer the object of pilgrimage. One day a small child with a bum unequal to the task sank down inside it, doubling up like a folding ruler, and got stuck. The trauma of the child's extraction put all the others off the thunderbox for a while. Then scatology itself became less engrossing than it had been for them, and the contraption was relegated to the barn, where it became a favourite nesting place for the bantams.

Opposite: *Plan for my replacement toolshed*

The privy made an ideal toolshed. Because it was too small to be a general dumping ground, it did not

A TOOL SHED FOR ANNA PAVORD, SHOWN
BY NO MEANS FULLY OCCUPIED

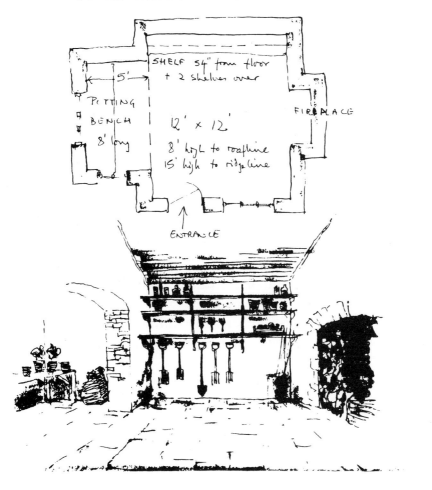

SHELF 54" from floor
+ 2 shelves over

5'

POTTING
BENCH
8' long

FIREPLACE

12' x 12'

8' high to roofline
15' high to ridgeline

ENTRANCE

need clearing out very often. It was close to the back door so, given a happy fifteen-minute break, I could nip out of the one door and into the other without being confronted by half a dozen other things that I ought to be doing on the way. Being stone and slate like the house, it was unassuming, a natural growth, and demanded nothing by way of maintenance or attention. The walls, as in the rest of the house, were 18in/45cm thick all round.

I speak of it in the past tense because, as a toolshed, it is now dead and gone. Incandescent with the white heat of technology, we have decided to install a boiler in the house, together with a few radiators in those rooms farthest away from the Aga. Until now, this has been the only permanent source of heat. But a boiler needs feeding and, as there is no gas in the village, we chose oil. Therefore there had to be a tank. I could choose, the plumber said magnanimously, between a site on top of my cyclamen bed or one inside the shed. I could have moved the cyclamen, but not even Helmut Newton could make a full frontal of an oil tank a feast for the eye. Losing the toolshed was the lesser of two evils.

Since that traumatic occasion, I have been wandering around with an armful of hoes, looking for a home for them. Of course, I do not need an armful of hoes – to tell the truth, I only ever use one of them, a small-headed Dutch hoe that is useful for worrying the earth around rows of young vegetables. None of them was bought. The most fearsome of the collection came from my great-uncle's shed, two hefty mattocks, a pronged cultivator and a massive hoe that could only be used by a gardener with forearms like Desperate Dan's. I feel constrained to keep these, because my great-uncle was a magnificent gardener. His tools are talismans.

Two other hoes we found here. One was propped against the window of the stables, and we discovered too late that it had more than a casual function. It was the only thing keeping the window frame attached to the wall. The second was buried in a mass of fecund nettles growing where we eventually made a vegetable patch.

Neither of these could go. They are part of the archaeology of the place, dispatches from long-lost inhabitants like the bottles, spoons, buttons and inkwells that we dig up in the garden, the messages scrawled in pencil on the stable stalls, the ancient initials scratched into the window panes. The hoes must be found the right resting place, and so far they have been unenthusiastic about any of the bowers I have shown them.

Another problem is posed by a crumbling shopping basket, patched up with string, which contains a potent collection of ancient poisons, none of them purchased by me. This basket – and its contents –

OCTOBER

was left behind in the toolshed by the previous occupants of our first house. Being then new to gardening,
I hung on to it, feeling that one day I should know
what all the bottles were for.

I have never learnt, but am now disinclined to
dump them for fear of some ghastly chemical genie
being released to poison the earth. Shortly after the
basket came to its present home in the privy/
toolshed, a blackbird built a nest on top of it and
raised three fledglings. The image of the nest balanced on top of the bottles of poison was straight
from the hippie sixties. Make love, not war.

What I liked most about the old shed was that it
grew into its role without any fussy interference on
my part. Rakes were balanced easily on the small lip
of wall under the eaves. Billhooks could safely be
jammed in the space between the rafters and the tiles.
There were enough large nails already poking out
from the woodwork to accommodate the forks, spades
and clippers that I used regularly. Plant pots and seed
trays were stacked against the back wall of the shed.

When I eventually light on a new headquarters for
the tools, I fear that I will not get off so easily.
Decisions will have to be made. Hoes in rows? Or
bunched together in a corner, as they always have
been? Tools hung in graduated order of height?
Altogether too much like the parade ground. And
the more organized the toolshed is, the more incum-

bent it will be upon me to retain that order.

Shock, horror – perhaps the cold utilitarianism of a new toolshed will force me to throw things away, to evaluate seriously the little hanks of string, pieces of wire, binder twine and skipping rope looped over the nails that do not hold tools. They are none of them essential, but together provide a comfortably familiar landscape, like the postcards you stick behind pots on the mantelpiece, and which imperceptibly become part of the wallpaper background.

I should, of course, take a firm grip on myself and throw away anything that I have not touched for the last five years. Housing the remaining skeleton collection would be no problem at all. I have, however, just got rid of a gardening jacket that has been my friend for eighteen years, and, recklessly, a clock that had lost some vital part of its innards. Surely no more sacrifices can be expected.

A good assortment of tools, used or not, is like protective clothing for the gardener. Golfers always have far more clubs about their person than they can possibly use. Rock musicians barricade themselves behind a phalanx of guitars. Why should I not have my daisy grubber and long-handled pruner, my brass hand syringe and selection of roses from the spouts of vanished watering cans? Meanwhile, I *must* find a home for this heterogeneous troupe. I have an awful feeling the hoes have designs on my study.

OCTOBER

THE POTAGER: PART TWO
A Neat Green Box for your Beds

To furnish a potager, you will need three different sorts of plants: some to edge the beds, some to fill them and some to give height, whether on their own legs (as, for example, standard gooseberries or bays) or borrowed ones, trained over an arbour or arch.

At the outset, you will have to decide which are going to have the upper hand – vegetables or flowers – and make your lists accordingly. Avoid too many permanent plantings of perennials, which will cut down your options for change. Iris can be accommodated in a potager and look at home there, but it is not the place for lupins or delphiniums. Avoid, too, plants such as alchemilla, which will try to take over the whole thing for themselves.

The vegetables that you choose should be decorative as well as edible. Asparagus is decorative, but takes up too much space to earn its keep in a potager only 16ft/5m square. Artichokes also need space, but you can make a meal from one artichoke – impossible from one spear of asparagus. An artichoke would make a good focal point if you have chosen a design that calls out for one. It is the most sculptural of all vegetables, with greyish, jagged leaves that splay out from the central crown. Intensely cold winters do it in, but not so often as to be disheartening. 'Vert de

Laon' or 'Camus de Bretagne' are the best for flavour.

Filler plants will be the subject of November's pot-ager planning. Edging plants are the ones we concen-trate on here. They need to be compact. Floppers will block the paths and swish wetly round your ankles; if they flop the other way they will smother crops. Traditional potagers have box-edged beds. In design terms, this is an advantage. The lines are clearly marked out. Box's evergreenness adds solidity and unifies the whole structure.

The disadvantage, in a small space, is that box is unproductive and greedy. Chives are a good alternative, though they dive underground for the winter. So is parsley, though you will have to renew it every couple of years. Thyme is also a possibility, but go for the bushy, shrubby kind, rather than a creeping variety. Thyme resents other plants lolling over it. It also needs full sun, which chives and parsley can do without.

Avoid mint, which will run all over the place. You could try basil, but it is slow to bulk up to a reasonable-sized plant and quick to turn up its toes at the first sign of cold. If you want to experiment, use the neat, bushy, small-leaved Greek variety. Winter savory (*Satureja montana*), like thyme, can be a per-manent fixture. It is shrubby, almost evergreen and remains at about 12in/30cm tall.

The temptation is to cram in as many different flowers and vegetables as you can, but the pattern of

OCTOBER

the potager will be most effective if you restrict your choice. Stick to perhaps four edgers, or fewer, and use them to enhance the symmetry of the layout.

When you are planning the planting, you will have to take the decision whether you are edging paths or beds. If paths, it is pleasant to have the same plant down both sides of it. This may mean that your bed has two different plants on two different sides. Not all paths need be of equal importance. You can highlight this by the way that you plant them.

Take design No. 5 on page 209. Here you might use chives along the paths from corners to centre, making them the main focus of the pattern. You could use parsley along either side of the four shorter paths to the centre and a flowery edging such as Spanish daisy (*Erigeron karvinskianus*) around the central square, where you might have a seat.

Herbs are only one of the edging options. You could also use alpine strawberries, with leaves that are good-looking over a long season. If you do this, choose a variety such as 'Baron Solemacher' that clumps rather than sends out runners. You never get anything approaching a meal from alpine strawberries, but they look pretty sprinkled on top of other fruit and provide elevenses when you are working in the potager.

You can also use flowers. The smaller violas make excellent edging plants and, if regularly dead-headed, are improvidently generous with flowers. 'Moonlight' has pale cream flowers, 'Baby Lucia' sky-blue ones, 'Haslemere' dirty pink. Avoid the trickier kinds, such as 'Irish Molly'. All violas do best in soil that is both moist and rich. The advantage of all this tribe is that they will do as well in half shade as in sun. Thrift and dianthus, also potential borderers, both need sun.

Some annuals make pleasant edgings, but do not give such a substantial air as chives or parsley. It is tempting to try and get the best of both worlds by interplanting, say, lobelia and chives, but again, restraint gives the better effect. Your edging will already be contrasting with whatever plants are filling in the beds. That is enough.

Flowery edgings are useful for the centre of a design and act as a foil to the excessive leafiness of vegetables such as lettuce. A bed of crinkly 'Lollo Rossa' edged with pale blue lobelia would be charming. Or leeks set round with the daisy-flowered erigeron.

The fat double daisy *Bellis perennis* is also a natural edger, though it needs to be used in tandem with another plant like the erigeron that picks up flowering where the bellis leaves off, in July. Ageratum, though sometimes slow to get into its stride, also has the neat habit of growth necessary for good edging.

Choose edgings, not only for their own merits, but also bearing in mind what you want to put in the bed behind. At the very least, the plants need to

OCTOBER

235

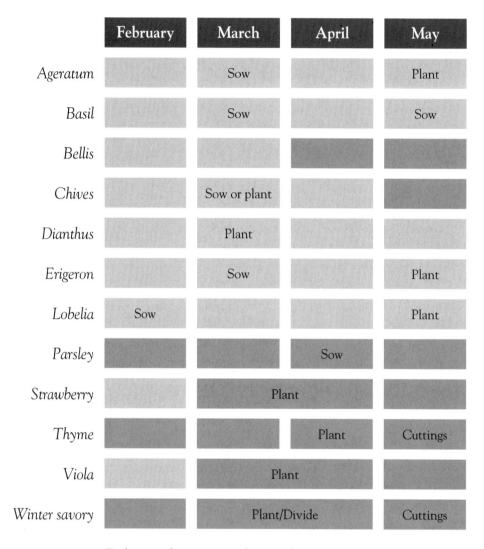

	February	March	April	May
Ageratum		Sow		Plant
Basil		Sow		Sow
Bellis				
Chives		Sow or plant		
Dianthus		Plant		
Erigeron		Sow		Plant
Lobelia	Sow			Plant
Parsley			Sow	
Strawberry		Plant		
Thyme			Plant	Cuttings
Viola		Plant		
Winter savory		Plant/Divide		Cuttings

Darker tint shows season of interest/cropping time

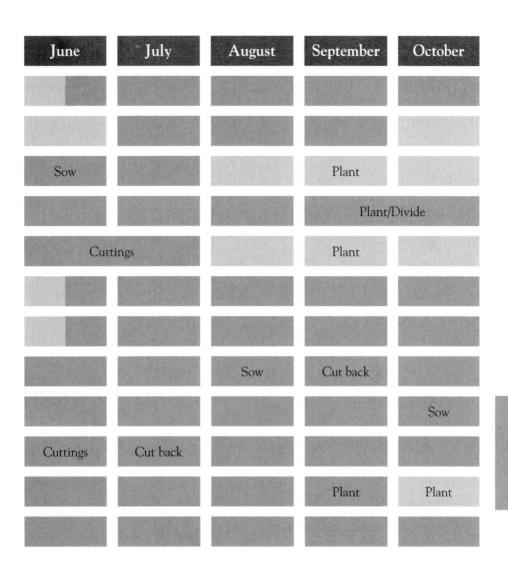

June	July	August	September	October
Sow			Plant	
			Plant/Divide	
Cuttings			Plant	
		Sow	Cut back	
				Sow
Cuttings	Cut back			
			Plant	Plant

accommodate each other's behaviour. Aim higher than that. Choose neighbours that set each other off well, that contrast in texture and form as well as colour.

Good edging plants include ageratum, basil, *Bellis* (double daisy), *Dianthus* (pink), erigeron, thyme and winter savory. However, chives, lobelia, parsley, strawberry and viola are firmly in the First Division.

Best Plants for Edging

Chives: Can be raised from seed sown in March but the simpler, though more expensive, option is to buy pot-grown plants and set them out, about 12in/30cm apart, in spring or autumn. Do not let them dry out. They like moist soil and full sun or half shade. The flower heads in June and July are decorative, but slow down leaf production. Nip some of them off. Divide congested clumps every four years in September or October. Chives spend winter underground, reappearing in March. *Action*: Buy plants in spring.

Lobelia: Common but never hackneyed, and like most perennials that we treat as annuals, flowering for a long season. Plants of 'Cambridge Blue' that I raised from seed this spring are still flowering outside in October. Frost will eventually be their downfall. A single colour will be better for edging than the mixtures offered in seed catalogues. 'Cambridge Blue' is sky-coloured. There are dark blue kinds with equally dark leaves. Trailing varieties can also be used for edging and they give a billowy effect, if that is what you want. Sow seed thinly on the surface of moist compost any time between late January and March. Cover with clear polythene. Germination takes some 2–3 weeks at room temperature (66–75°F/ 19–24°C). The seedlings are tiny. Prick out in small clumps rather than singly. *Action*: Sow seed January-March, buy plantlets in April or fully grown bedding plants in May.

Parsley: The curly-leaved types make the prettiest edgings. The flat-leaved French type has the best flavour. Sow seed outside in March-April or July-August. It is extremely slow to germinate. Soaking the seed for 24 hours before sowing sometimes helps. Mix radish seed with the parsley to give a swifter effect. As you eat the radish, you will be thinning the parsley rows. Parsley needs fertile soil but will grow in sun or half shade. Cut down the stems in September to promote fresh growth. Some people report success in transplanting supermarket parsley from punnet to the open ground. It is certainly worth a try. *Action*: Sow seed March-April or try punnet transplants in spring.

Strawberry: Only alpine types are suitable for edging. 'Baron Solemacher' has the extra advantage of not making runners. It makes a mound of handsome bright green foliage with fruit in late summer and autumn. Alpine strawberries can be raised from seed sown in boxes in autumn and overwintered in a cold frame. As with chives, the simpler method is to buy pot-grown plants and put them out about 18in/45cm apart. **Action**: Buy plants in spring.

Viola: Irresistible, long-flowering plants in a wide range of colours. 'Chantreyland' is apricot, 'Vita' an elegant shade of mauve. (Well, it would be, wouldn't it?) Regular dead-heading prolongs the display. Easy, trouble-free plants thriving in moist soil in sun or half shade. Can be raised from seed sown in a box in a shaded cold frame in July or early August. Simpler to buy ready-grown plants. You can get them in strips, like bedding plants. Cut back long exhausted stems in July to encourage fresh growth from the centre of the plant. **Action**: Buy plants in spring.

Jobs for the Month

General

❀ Lay new turf now so that the grass can settle during the winter.

❀ A collection of different mints can be difficult to control. Punch or burn holes in the bottom of a number of big square ice-cream or margarine containers and plant a different mint in each box. Sink the boxes under the earth.

❀ Wash the shading off the greenhouse and insulate it with bubble polythene.

❀ Gather up autumn leaves and stack them in an enclosure of wire netting to rot down into leafmould. This makes a superb mulch.

❀ Leaves in garden pools are a bad thing. Catch them as they fall by stretching netting over the pool.

❀ Trees are best planted any time between now and Christmas.

Flowers

❀ Continue to plant daffodils, scattering bonemeal into the planting holes. A long-handled bulb planter that takes out neat plugs of earth is the easiest tool to use when planting daffodils in turf.

❀ Puschkinia and *Anemone blanda* will both naturalize successfully and should be planted now. Puschkinia can be planted in short grass, rockeries or in the front of a border.

❀ Finish planting spring bedding such as wallflowers, polyanthus and forget-me-nots. The latter make an excellent undercarpet for tulips, especially the dark mahogany 'Abu Hassan' or the lily-flowered 'White Triumphator'.

❀ Martagon lily is a hardy lime-tolerant basal-rooting species that will thrive in sun or shade. Plant the bulbs about 4in/10cm deep and 9in/23cm apart on a sprinkle of sharp sand to deter underground slugs. Mulch in spring with compost or leafmould.

❀ Start to overhaul herbaceous borders, changing any groupings of plants that have put your teeth on edge during the summer. Split up congested clumps and replant them in soil refreshed with compost or bonemeal.

❀ October is a bad month for gales so check the ties on wall shrubs and climbers.

❀ Some alpine plants, particularly those with woolly leaves, need protection from excessive damp during the winter. A dressing of stone chippings will help rain to drain away fast.

❀ Leave dahlias and begonias in the ground as long as possible before lifting: tubers do most of their growing in the short days of autumn. Lift them only when the foliage has been blackened by the first frosts. Cut the stems off about 4in/10cm above the ground and stack the tubers upside down in boxes to dry out. Store them in a frost-free shed.

* Frost also stops tender fuchsias in their tracks. Shift them in their pots into a frost-free shed or porch for the winter.

* Lift pelargoniums that you want to keep and stack them in boxes of peat in a cool, frost-free place. Do not water, but allow the leaves to die off naturally. Wrap the rootballs in polythene bags with a little damp peat. Tie the bags in bundles and hang them up until spring.

* Windowboxes need clearing of summer displays ready for planting with winter pansies or bulbs such as low-growing crocus and irises. Variegated ivies are excellent gap fillers for winter months.

Vegetables

* Lift main-crop carrots, if the kitchen garden is inconveniently far from the back door. They store well in bags of slightly damp sand or peat stacked in a cool place.

* Cut down the dead brown stems of asparagus fern and clean up the beds. Put markers in any space where you may need fresh plants.

* Spread muck thickly over at least a third of the vegetable garden after ground has been cleared and roughly dug. The muck can be dug in in spring when it has weathered.

* In a greenhouse continue to sow special winter-hardy lettuce.

Fruit

* Clean up the ground between strawberry rows, getting rid of weeds and unwanted plants that may have rooted themselves. Mulch between the rows with well-rotted compost or manure.

* Many apples and pears are now ready for picking. Temperature is the most critical factor in successful storage. It should be 36–41°F/2–5°C. Somewhere dark and slightly damp is ideal.

* Put greasebands round the trunks of fruit trees to trap the crawling, wingless winter moths whose progeny may cause havoc among the fruit next season.

Propagating

* Pot up rooted cuttings of zonal and ivy-leaved pelargoniums, so that the plants have a chance to develop a decent root system before winter sets in.

* Take cuttings of gooseberry, redcurrant and blackcurrant. Use pencil-thick growths, about 12in/30cm long.

NOVEMBER

WEASEL WORDS

Seduction by catalogue creates pitfalls for the unwary gardener. The problem – as ever – lies in the gap between promise and performance. In this season of lists and mega wilfulness, it is easy to be led astray. Beginners particularly need to hone an ability to read between the lines.

'Seeds itself about very happily' seems a harmless enough characteristic in a plant, even a generous one. But for this, read 'quickly becomes a pest'. You can have too much of anything, especially alchemilla, one of the greatest culprits on this score. There is a way round this problem: cut off the flower heads before they run to seed. Such counsel of perfection rarely prevails. No garden should be without alchemilla, but no gardener should be unaware of its intense desire to perpetuate itself.

Brunnera, with handsome rough heart-shaped leaves and sprays of forget-me-not blue flowers in spring, is another vigorously fecund plant. Both it and alchemilla are surprisingly difficult to dig up once established. Self-seeding in annuals is less of a problem since they are, anyway, transient passengers.

'Resents disturbance'. This suggests a sulker, quite likely to die in transit, even more likely to die when you decide, as is usually the case after its first season, that you have put it in the wrong place. I don't blame plants for resenting disturbance. I resent disturbance, but it makes for a slow sort of garden if too many of your plants are kicking their heels, being resentful. Peonies are culprits here, and certain sorts of iris, such as the tall, graceful *Iris chrysographes*.

The opposite of this is 'a wonderful doer'. This usually turns out to be a dangerous thug which gallops over the ground at an impossible rate, squashing less robust neighbours without compunction. If you have a horrible corner of ground, builder's rubble, solid yellow clay or infested with weeds, you could turn it into a thug's corner. Plant several wonderful doers together and let them slug it out over twenty rounds. In mixed plantings they need to be treated as brutally as they behave, rigorously chopped and contained.

Most comfreys come into this category, especially the low-growing *Symphytum grandiflorum*. Some thugs are so good-looking that, in spite of past experience, you succumb. I have just planted another *Symphytum × uplandicum* 'Variegatum', one of a family of tall comfreys, introduced originally from Russia as fodder plants. This particular type has bold creamy-white margins to its leaves and the usual hairy sprays of blue-purple flowers. Its companions, a choisya and a *Cercis siliquastrum* are, I hope, now tough enough to be able to stand up to their new neighbour.

In certain sorts of catalogues, usually those specializing in hardy plants or unusual bulbs, you find

NOVEMBER

a different class of phrase. You may read of flowers 'nestling among the leaves' or 'intriguingly splashed with écru and chocolate'. Either way, the flowers will be invisible, but to a certain class of gardener, this does not matter. You may find yourself being drawn inexorably into this happy, myopic band. Before you are, be warned that here 'choice' and 'very choice' mean expensive or very expensive. 'Highly sought after' means the same thing.

Sometimes the nerves of even these hardy planters fail and they can find nothing more to say about their charge than 'an interesting plant'. This usually signifies that it is indistinguishable from a weed, but has been collected high up on the Cerro Catedral, which makes it an ultra-snob plant. And there is joy in becoming the only person to succeed with a plant which nature never intended for a rockery in Ewell. This thrill should not be underestimated.

Plants described as 'useful ground cover' are only suitable for those who loathe gardening and are looking for nothing more than a greenish equivalent of concrete. The Rose of Sharon, *Hypericum calycinum*, is a typical example of this. It is a sub-shrub, spreading by means of wiry, underground stolons. It has tough, leathery leaves and yellow flowers in the second half of summer. I loathe it with a passion and have been trying for years to eradicate it from its hold under a beech tree in my own garden. It seems to

shrug off glyphosate and is adept at bobbing up from bits of root that you miss when you try to dig it up.

Anything labelled as useful ground cover will prove equally difficult to despatch. The silver-leaved dead nettle, *Lamium galeobdolon*, is another leech of this kind, though a prettier one than the dirty, dusty carpeter of roundabouts and crematorium forecourts, the Rose of Sharon.

'Irresistible' plants were recently hostas and are probably now salvias. Some plants *are* irresistible, but it is better to trust your own judgement in this matter than that of the catalogue writer. See the thing before you plunge.

The most irresistible plant I bought recently was a *Cercis canadensis* 'Forest Pansy', but it is not described as such in Hillier's catalogue. 'Flowers magenta in bud,' they say coolly, 'opening pale pink before heart-shaped reddish purple leaves, which retain their colour throughout summer.' I saw it in a Cornish garden and scribbled its name in the back of a diary, heavily underlined and circled. It seemed hideously expensive, but worth every penny. It holds itself elegantly, the leaves drooping slightly from the branches. The newest leaves are the most highly polished and the reddest. I have not had any flowers yet (the thing scarcely needs them), but I have given it some colchicums underneath for company.

If you are a collector by nature – of hostas, salvias,

NOVEMBER

gladioli or begonias – you will not need to be told that something is irresistible. If it is a new introduction, you will buy it anyway, because that is what collectors do. I like a plant to have something more than newness to offer. Flower size or colour are sometimes achieved at the expense of the plant's overall health and vigour. I don't want to be nursemaid to beds of invalids.

'Needs careful placing' is a phrase that is often attached to new plants. This has more to do with the plant's neighbours than its own needs. It generally means that the colour is unbelievably awful, forcing you to remain hypnotically locked on to it at the expense of the rest of the garden. There is a shade of salmon that always needs careful placing – on the bonfire.

If you come across phrases like 'darling flowers dancing like dragonflies over dewy foliage' there is no option but to change catalogues. There is no shortage now, with the welcome explosion of small specialist nurseries listed in the invaluable reference book *The Plant Finder*, which gives sources for 50,000 different plants. You can order plants now to be delivered in spring, when you will be feeling more like doing something with them.

As seducers, catalogues are not quite what they used to be. The recession has seen to that. The best of the old ones I kept from my great-uncle's bookshelves have the qualities of the small private presses of the 1930s: thick paper, superb typography and, if you are lucky, illustrations. You take for granted their horticultural expertise.

Even in the pinched year of 1950, the Blackmoor Estate's catalogue of selected fruit trees had an expensively engraved cover and generous wide margins on all its thick pages. My great-uncle ordered twenty-three kinds of apples for a new orchard and used the margins to scribble robust notes to himself.

Scotts Nurseries of Merriott, Somerset, until recently kept up the tradition of good-looking catalogues. Theirs always contained gorgeous work by the engraver Robin Tanner, as well as invaluable written information for gardeners, particularly in the case of fruit. Scotts' catalogues also contain thumbnail sketches showing the habit of plants, a practice that should be much more widely taken up. It is so much easier to choose, say, a viburnum if you can open the page and see immediately that 'Lanarth', which you liked the sound of when you read the description, is actually going to be much too wide for your purpose, or *Viburnum davidii* too low. When you are experienced, you can visualize these things in your head from the description and the dimensions given. When you are beginning, it is difficult.

Generous catalogues give you as much information, not only about the plants themselves but

NOVEMBER

about ways of using them, as you would find in any gardening book. Notcutts' hefty catalogue is excellent in this respect. So is Beth Chatto's brilliant list from her nursery Unusual Plants. The best catalogue, however, is hopeless unless it can be followed up with good plants.

~✦~

In Praise of Boris Parsnip

Nobody writes poems about parsnips. Nor do you find chefs clucking and fussing over them in expensive restaurants. Courgettes have all the fun, primped out in a hundred different ways. Parsnips rarely crawl out from their traditional berth, tucked under the Sunday roast. Try this recipe instead. It is from *The Cook's Garden* by Linda Brown.

You will need 1½lb/700g parsnips, a large cooking apple, the juice of half a lemon and a couple of teaspoons of brown sugar. Cook the parsnips in as little water as you can manage. Purée them and spread half the mixture over a gratin dish. Cover with half the apple slices. Repeat the process with the rest of the parsnip and apple. Sprinkle the lemon juice and sugar over the top and bake in a medium oven (350–375°F/180–190°C/gas mark 4–5) for about half an hour. This will feed two hungry people or three on diets.

This might make you feel more interested in parsnips. It might even make you feel poetic. It was Jane Grigson who pointed out that the Russian for parsnip was *pasternak*. Would we feel the same way about *Dr Zhivago* if we knew it had been written by Boris Parsnip? It just shows how low the vegetable has sunk in our esteem.

For me, however, this has been the winter of the parsnip, thanks to a bumper crop, only improved by frosty weather. Cold intensifies the flavour of parsnips and converts some of their starch into sugar so that they are sweeter in cold winters than in mild ones.

The seed went in on 24 April. This is right at the end of the recommended time, but late sowings germinate faster than early ones and there is no particular advantage – unless you are a showman – in having early crops. The parsnip, though deeply comforting in winter, is not something you ever think of eating in summer.

The variety I used was 'White King' from Van Hage. Later, when the seedlings were well established, they were thinned out. The usual instruction is to leave 6–9in/15–23cm between each one. Mine are probably more like 4–6in/10–15cm apart, because I do not want monsters. Huge parsnips are difficult to dig up and peeling them is like painting the Forth Bridge. The thinning is important, though it seems wasteful, but it will be the only attention

NOVEMBER

your parsnips need, apart from the general hoeing that goes on in vegetable beds to keep down weeds.

Situation is important. It needs to be open, and the soil on the dryish side when you sow. Seed has to be fresh. Some vegetable seed can be kept from year to year with no appreciable effect on germination rates. Not parsnip. Like most root vegetables, they do best in deep but light soil. Do not grow them in ground that has been very recently manured (unless, of course, you have your eye on the 'rudest root' class at your local horticultural show). Canker is their only enemy. This usually shows as reddish-brown, sometimes black, patches on the roots, especially at the shoulders. Sometimes it spreads through the whole of the parsnip, but usually the patches are small enough to be cut away when you are preparing the roots. There is no effective remedy, but fortunately many varieties are now bred to be resistant to the disease.

'Cobham Improved' is canker-resistant and won an Award of Merit in the Royal Horticultural Society's vegetable trials at Wisley. So did 'Javelin' and Marshall's strain of the well-known variety 'Tender and True'. You can get 'Cobham Improved' from Carters, Dobies and Marshalls.

This information is miraculously at my fingertips thanks to *The Vegetable Finder*, produced by the Henry Doubleday Research Association. This booklet is modelled on the well-known *Plant Finder* and lists all available varieties of vegetables together with details of who sells what. I was delighted to find thirty-one different kinds of parsnips to explore. For half of them there was only one source of supply.

The tenuous hold on survival that haunts many varieties of vegetables is what strikes you about this list. We all like to feel we understand about the importance of genetic diversity, but if we all continue only to buy one of the four most popular varieties of parsnip ('Avonresister', 'Hollow Crown', 'Tender and True' and 'White Gem') we are doing nothing in a practical sense to ensure that diversity.

Those four parsnips are not popular without a reason. They have proved themselves over a long period. You will find 'Hollow Crown' recommended in gardening books written a hundred years ago. But the saying about eggs in baskets goes for vegetables too. If the genetic base dwindles to four varieties, you are short of building blocks when the need arises to build a new variety resistant to some as yet unsuspected disease.

Alan Gear, head of the HDRA, draws a parallel with rare breeds of farm animal. 'They have been found to possess qualities required by today's consumer. Had they not been kept going by dedicated enthusiasts belonging to the Rare Breeds Survival Trust, those genetic lines would have gone for ever.'

NOVEMBER

And for town dwellers, a parsnip is a great deal easier to keep than a Soay sheep.

The problems began in the seventies, when new EEC legislation required that all varieties offered for sale be officially registered. This involved not only endless form-filling but also cash: £1,800 to register a variety, plus £400 each year to keep it on the official list. Seedsmen run businesses, not charities. If nobody buys the more unusual varieties, they can hardly be expected to maintain them.

The Vegetable Finder lists 2,802 different varieties of vegetables, which sounds comforting, but 60 per cent of them are stocked by only one seedsman. These, obviously, are the ones that are in most danger of disappearing. So this spring, adopt a pea. Instead of growing 'Kelvedon Wonder', a variety which is supplied by 26 seedsmen, try 'Dark Skinned Perfection', which has only one supplier, R.V. Roger of Pickering.

My first sowing of peas last year (also 24 April) was a disaster. The rooks learned to tweak them out of the ground when they had just germinated, and polished off the row before I realized what was going on. The second sowing (30 May) was more successful, using a new variety, 'Minnow', from Dobies. This grows *petit pois* peas, eight or so packed together in stumpy pods. It was easy and prolific; also short – only 2ft/60cm high – which makes support easier.

British Leyland

There are many reasons not to plant × *Cupresso-cyparis leylandii*, the Leyland cypress. It is character-less. It is depressing. It is like a cuckoo in the nest. It almost always outgrows its home, engaging its keepers in an exhausting battle with shears, loppers and saw to keep its greedy branches from taking all light and space to itself. Few trees look as uncomfortable in our landscape as the Leyland cypress. There are just two places where I have seen it looking at home: in a cemetery and screening an electricity sub-station.

Leylands do not change with the seasons. They have no blossom and no fruit to speak of. There is neither shape nor shine to the leaf, and no architec-ture about the things at all.

What they *can* do is grow, sometimes up to 2ft/ 60cm a year. If you are fighting to establish some privacy in a pocket handkerchief of a plot surrounded by nosy neighbours, this may seem a great advantage. And so it is, for the first three years or so. After that, it is a curse. For each extra couple of feet that the thing reaches into the sky, there is a corresponding shadow on the ground. It does not take long before the whole handkerchief may be cast in gloom, con-fined in a suffocating, dark green prison.

There is a small brick cottage that I used to pass every week on my way to town. It sat in the middle of a small field hedged round with the usual country mixture of blackthorn, field maple, hazel and ash. After almost a hundred years of unpretentious life as a farm worker's cottage, it was sold for improvement.

Plastic windows replaced the wooden casements and the Welsh slate roof made way for Marley tiles of an uncompromising colour, but it was the day the bulldozers moved in to grub out the old hedge that I felt like throwing myself in the juggernauts' path.

None of my business, I know. An Englishman's home is his castle. But why murder a perfectly good hedge at great expense to plant instead hideous lines of Leyland cypress that look as at home in the country as heifers in Piccadilly? 'Die, you beasts, die,' I used to mutter vindictively as I drove past each week. They have not, but the cottage has not sold. Perhaps there is a moral in this tale after all.

Hoping that I may be witnessing the beginning of a reaction against the dreaded conifer, I hurried along to the local garden centre to check out sales figures for Leyland cypress. 'Definitely our best line,' said the foreman, depressingly. 'People like it because it is a good, fast grower.' Why should fast growth automatically be an advantage, I wonder? Instant gardening is no more satisfying to the soul than thirty-second snatches of Mozart, condensed novels or fast food.

If there is a horrible view at the bottom of your garden, that you want to get rid of quickly, do not plant Leyland cypress. You will merely get another horrible view. Since the spread of a mature tree is around 15ft/5m, you will also lose a lot of your garden.

Think instead of putting up some form of fence topped with trellis that you can then clothe with a variety of scramblers: nasturtium, canary creeper, cobaea and morning glory for colour, ivies and *Akebia quinata* for evergreen foliage.

If you have a plot surrounded by the chain-link fence so beloved of developers intent on maximizing profit, clothe it in ivy or smother it with roses. The cluster-flowered climbers such as 'Wedding Day' and 'Rambling Rector' flower freely with bunches of creamy, heavily scented flowers followed by tiny hips. They have long whippy growths which can easily be tied in horizontally along a fence.

If you are adamant about a hedge of some sort, think carefully about what you want it to do. For a stock-proof, dog-proof, vandal-proof hedge, there is nothing to beat thorn, either hawthorn (*Crataegus monogyna*) with masses of scented white flowers in May and red berries in autumn, or blackthorn (*Prunus spinosa*), armed with vicious spikes but bearing delicate white flowers in April, followed by sloes in autumn, useful if you have a weakness for sloe gin (as we saw in September).

For a classic hedge, there is little to equal beech,

NOVEMBER

257

especially if you slide the odd holly and copper beech in among the standard variety to vary the texture. Beech hedges hang on to their leaves in winter, which is useful.

Any of these solutions will be kinder on the eye than the Leyland cypress, and not much tougher on the pocket. Even if you plant 2ft/60cm tall Leylands, they will still be expensive. If you are the impatient kind who goes for 3ft/90cm trees, the price becomes prohibitive. For almost a quarter of that you can buy 2ft/60cm hedging beech, though of course you will need more of them, as they must be planted closer together than Leylands. Hawthorn is even cheaper.

THE POTAGER: PART THREE
SHORT-STAY BEDS FOR WELL-MATCHED COUPLES

The plants that you use to fill the beds of your potager should not, in the main, be permanent fixtures. Flexibility gives you a greater choice of crops. It suits the soil, too. When you clear away a crop of beans, or marigolds, you have a chance to fork over and feed the soil. Potagering is an intensive form of gardening. You can't continue to take from the soil without giving it something back in return.

Aim, when you are choosing filler plants, for a reasonable balance between flowers and vegetables.

Avoid vegetables such as broad beans and Brussels sprouts. They are far too butch for this sort of boudoir gardening. Some cabbages – the red kind, and the ornamental kales – adapt well, but have a long grow-ing season. If you do not have a patch of ground where you can bring vegetables on before transplant-ing them into the ornamental potager, this will limit your choice.

There are ways of having flowers and vegetables together in the same plot. If you do this, choose a plain border such as chives or parsley to go round the bed, otherwise it will all look too frantic. Restraint (difficult in a small garden when you want to try as many new plants as possible) is the keynote of most successful potagers.

Oriental saladini is an ideal potager crop and can be used as a catch-crop while you are waiting for slower-growing plants to develop. Or you can use it in a bed of its own, mixing the seed with a packet of nigella or love-in-a-mist before you sow it.

You need to be aware what seedling nigellas look like so you can avoid them while you are picking the saladini. Fortunately, they are distinctive, with very feathery leaves. If you are really worried about making mistakes, sow a few seeds separately in a pot to show you what to avoid.

The saladini is a mixture of five vegetables. At the seedling stage they make brilliant winter salads. You

NOVEMBER

do not pull the plants up wholesale, but nip young leaves here and there as the plants grow. Later, if you want, you can transplant some of the seedlings into a separate bed to grow into full-blown plants. Mizuna, one of the saladini ingredients, is particularly pretty with deeply cut, fern-like leaves and would look excellent used this way in a potager.

Pak choi, komatsuna, Santo loose-leaved cabbage and purple mustard are the other ingredients of the mixture sold by Suffolk Herbs. You can make your own mixtures, but to do so, you will have to spend more on seed. Joy Larkcom's book *Oriental Vegetables* tells you everything you need to know about them.

For the purposes of a potager, autumn sowing of the mixture will give you a non-stop supply of unusual winter salad, just as the lettuce begin to run out. This will also suit the nigella, if you decide to dress up the saladini with flowers. You will need roughly half an ounce of seed for each square yard or metre of bed. Broadcast the seed thinly on the surface of the soil and cover it lightly. If cats are a problem, cover the bed with netting. Germination of the salad is fast: you can start cutting it within a month.

For this purpose, avoid dwarf nigellas such as 'Dwarf Moody Blue'. It will get swamped by the greens. The standard variety, 'Miss Jekyll', gets to about 18in/45cm and flowers between June and September. Autumn sowing means that the flowers get into their stride more quickly.

In successful flower and vegetable combinations, the two need to be well matched in size and vigour. Carrots and cornflowers would work, again with a reasonably subdued edging. Carrots are very slow to germinate, but the taste of home-grown is so much better than bought, they are worth the space. Thompson & Morgan say their introduction, 'Bertan', is exceptionally sweet. It is ready to eat in autumn. 'Chantenay Red Cored' is a reliable standard variety which you sow in late April and early May to use by October or November.

This sowing date will suit the cornflowers, too. Here again, you need to avoid dwarfs. 'Blue Diadem' grows about 30in/75cm tall and has the biggest flowers of all the family. Mix the carrot and corn-flower seed together and broadcast it over the potager bed. For all seed sowing, the ground should be shuffled over and raked to firm it and smooth it. Cover the seed thinly with soil.

There are other ways to use flowers and vegetables together, taking advantage of their different seasons of growth. Tulips, for instance, are at their height at a time when few vegetables have got into their stride. In April or May they could hog a bed by themselves. Plant them close together for maximum effect. Later, use the bed for leeks.

You can buy leeks ready to transplant in early sum-

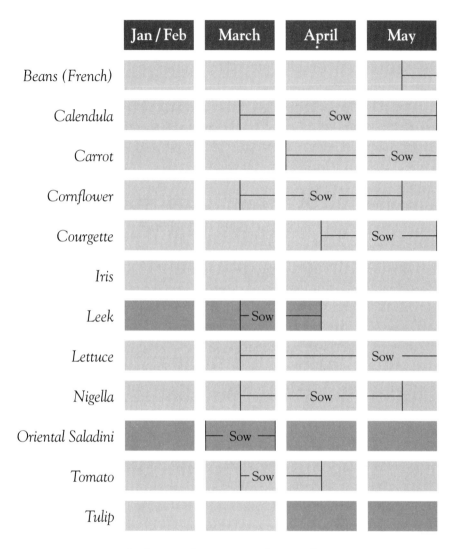

	Jan / Feb	March	April	May
Beans (French)				├──
Calendula		├──	── Sow	───
Carrot			├──	── Sow ──
Cornflower		├──	── Sow ──	┤
Courgette			├──	Sow ──
Iris				
Leek		├ Sow	├──	
Lettuce		├──	───	Sow ──
Nigella		├──	── Sow ──	┤
Oriental Saladini		├ Sow ──		
Tomato		├ Sow	──	
Tulip				

Darker tint shows season of interest/cropping time

June	July	August	September	October	Nov/Dec
Sow					
			Sow		
	Plant/Divide		Plant		
Plant					
			Sow		
			Sow		
Plant out					
					Plant

mer. If you have a spare piece of nursery ground, you can raise them yourself, sowing the seed in March and transplanting the young plants to the potager bed in late June or early July. Lift the tulips out of the bed before you fill it with leeks. Replanted among shrubs, some may flower again, but they are not as reliable in this respect as daffodils.

I sowed 'Musselburgh', an old leek variety from Unwins, on 30 March this year and have been using them for the past six weeks. It is an advantage to have a proportion of winter vegetables in your potager, and more pleasing to look on than bare earth.

You can make this tulip/leek bed work even harder by scattering eschscholzia seed over the ground as soon as you have lifted the tulips and before you plant the leeks. It is such a feathery thing, it will not get in the way of the vegetables, but it needs sun. It has silky poppyish flowers, orange in the standard type, but buff, pink and apricot as well in a Suttons' mixture called 'Ballerina'.

Tomatoes are favourite candidates for home growing. Choose outdoor varieties for a potager. I always grow bush tomatoes, which sprawl around on the ground, but where space is limited, upright kinds make better use of it. Then you could grow marigolds round the tomatoes' feet. Thompson & Morgan's 'Sweet 100' is one of the best for flavour with long trusses of cherry tomatoes like 'Gardener's Delight'.

Their 'Tigrella' has slightly larger fruit, red striped with yellow, and can crop earlier than 'Sweet 100'.

Tomatoes cannot go in the ground until the end of May, so these too could share a bed with early bulbs. The marigold (*Calendula*) seed can be scattered on the earth as soon as you have planted the tomatoes. You do not need to disturb the soil. Cover the seed with a sprinkling of compost instead. With regular dead-heading you will get a good show of flowers. I threw some of Suttons' 'Art Shades Mixed' marigold seed on a spare bit of ground on 13 June this year and they are still flowering (although tattily).

Bearded iris are one of the few permanent plantings to encourage in a potager. They flourish in beds on their own as the rhizomes like sunbathing. The foliage is good, too, if you can fend off leaf spot and rust. You may think irises are wasteful occupants of a potager bed, but think of the stunning display in June. Salve your conscience by sowing winter catch-crops of lamb's lettuce in between the rhizomes and by filling the bed with early *Crocus tommasinianus*.

Some crops, such as courgettes, are difficult to work in with other ingredients as they are greedy growers. No matter. Give them a bed of their own. Being frost-tender, they cannot go out until the end of May. For showiness choose a yellow-skinned form such as Marshalls' 'Gold Rush'.

French beans, always expensive to buy, are also an

ideal potager crop. Do not be tempted to plant them too early. The seeds sulk and rot in cold ground. 'Purple Tepee' from Thompson & Morgan is a handsome stringless variety with deep purple pods. They revert to green when you cook them. Marshalls' 'Delinel' is also excellent.

Lettuce are good not only for eating, but for texture and pattern in the potager. Choose several contrasting varieties, including perhaps the Cos type 'Little Gem' and the frilly 'Lollo Rossa'. There is no shortage of choice.

JOBS FOR THE MONTH

General

❧ Save the turf from planting holes cut for trees and shrubs in established lawns and set it, grass side down, in the bottom of the hole. As it rots it will provide humus to improve soil structure.

❧ Repair jobs on fences, trellises and boundary walls should be done through winter when climbers and wall shrubs are dormant and can easily be taken down from their supports.

❧ It is often difficult to water trees and shrubs planted on a steep slope. Plant an old drainpipe or plastic soft-drink bottle with both ends cut off alongside the tree. Set it so the top just surfaces above the soil. Water delivered through the pipe will get straight to the roots of the tree.

❧ Check newly planted evergreens for wind-rock. They offer far more wind resistance than deciduous trees and shrubs. Stamp down the soil round them so their roots can get a firm grip on it.

❧ Terracotta pots that have been standing in saucers of water all summer should now have those saucers removed. Pots are less likely to crack open in icy weather if the compost is well drained. Raise pots on small even blocks of wood to ease drainage problems. Where style is paramount, use terracotta lion's paws specially made for the job.

❧ If possible, order seeds this side of Christmas.

❧ Clean mowing machines after the last grass cut of the year. Wash off all mud and grass and cover all the important shiny-looking bits of the engine with a thin layer of oil or grease.

❧ Protect plants overwintering in cold frames by covering the glass with layers of sacking or hessian on frosty nights.

❧ Plant new hedges of deciduous trees.

❧ Overhaul water pumps used for fountains and waterfalls. Remove submersible pumps and store them safely.

Flowers

❧ Plant tulips at the beginning of the month. They are excellent in tubs. You can also use them in windowboxes, but choose the shorter varieties and those of the Greigii and Kaufmanniana families with striped and mottled leaves. Miniature tulips such as *T. tarda* or *T. turkestanica* are charming in troughs and rockeries.

❧ Cut back summer sprawlers such as mallow, reducing branches to the base. New growth will start in spring.

❧ Do not cut back slightly tender plants such as penstemon. They may put out fresh shoots which will get massacred by frosts.

🌺 Check that bulbs you are forcing inside for early flowering have not dried out. The compost should be just damp.

🌺 Draw the leaves over the crowns of slightly tender plants such as red hot pokers and tie them up in a bundle to provide winter protection.

🌺 Pile dry leaves on top of agapanthus and nerines for insulation.

🌺 Continue to cut down stems of late summer perennials such as Michaelmas daisy, golden rod and perennial verbascum. Mulch thickly round the clumps.

🌺 Plant new roses while growth is dormant. Climbing roses destined to grow against walls should be planted at least 15in/38cm away from the base of the wall. The soil closer to the wall will be too dry for the plant to thrive.

🌺 Put cloches or panes of glass over Christmas roses (*Helleborus niger*) to keep the flowers clean and free from splashes of earth.

🌺 Pick fallen leaves from rockeries where they may smother and rot alpine plants underneath. Top up the stone chippings around rock plants to improve drainage. Shelter lewisias with panes of glass.

🌺 Protect plants which are prone to frost damage (hardy fuchsia, *Ceratostigma willmottianum*, California tree poppy (*Romneya coulteri*) and solanum. Mulch all around the plants to insulate the roots with chipped bark, straw, leaves or bracken.

Vegetables

🌺 Plant garlic at the beginning of the month.

🌺 In warmer parts of the country, it is worth trying an early row of broad beans.

🌺 Sow an early row of round-seeded peas, such as 'Feltham First'.

🌺 Protect the crowns of globe artichokes with loosely packed straw or bracken.

🌺 Plant chicory roots in large pots containing sand, water them and put them somewhere cool and dark.

🌺 Harvest leeks and parsnips.

🌺 Lift and store beetroot and celeriac.

Fruit

🌺 Prune apple and pear trees after leaf fall. Cut out all dead, diseased or damaged branches and prune other growth selectively to eliminate crossing or rubbing branches.

🌺 Plant new raspberry canes 18in/45cm apart in rows 6ft/2m apart. Prune hard after planting.

🌺 Plant gooseberries, setting the bushes 5ft/1.5m apart.

DECEMBER

DIY CHRISTMAS

'I expect you are busy getting ready for Christmas,' people say to me at the beginning of November. I do not understand why Christmas is now turned into an eight-week endurance marathon, but my answer loud and clear is, 'No, I have not been getting ready for it.' It will start as it always does, no more than a week before, in a frantic flail of silver paint and ivy.

The first thing that gets done is always the wreath on the back door. These are very easy to make if you can get hold of a short length of chicken wire netting. Roll the wire into a rough tube about 3in/75mm in diameter and bend it round in a circle roughly 16in/40cm across. Wire the ends to stop the circle shape drifting apart.

Lay the wire circle on a table and tie a loop of wire round it for hanging it up. Cut short lengths of holly 4–5in/about 10cm long and jam them into the netting, working from the outside of the circle over the top to the inside. Push the stalks hard in so that the first pair of leaves is trapped in the wire. No sprig should stick out much more than its neighbour. If you have variegated holly you can make a pattern round the rim of the circle, contrasting with plain holly. You will be lucky to find any with berries on. I cheat and wire red baubles on to the wreath. Finish with a big bow of red ribbon, with the ends cut swallow-tail fashion to hang below the wreath.

You can also make wreaths from the long whippy growths pruned from a vine, or from stems of a rampant *Clematis montana* that needs cutting back, or from the wild clematis, old man's beard. Whatever you cut, take care to do it cleanly, using sharp secateurs or loppers. Cut off the branch you want at its junction with another stem so that you do not leave ugly snags. This is particularly important with holly, which often grows in a rather lax way. You may want only the last few inches of a twig, the bit with the leaves, but if you cut it in this way, you will leave an ugly framework of bare twigs. Take the whole thing off and trim what you need.

To make a wreath from vine or clematis, take a handful of long stems and tie them together, thick ends staggered so that they do not all end at exactly the same point. Twist the thick stems round each other as if you were making a rope, then use the thin ends to lash round the thicker ends until you have a rough circle of stem. This is the base. What you decorate it with depends on what is to hand and where it is to be used. Laid flat with candles in the middle it makes a good table centre, or it can be hung on the wall.

Everything will have to be wired on to a wreath of this sort. The stems are not secure enough to hold things fast. Clippings from the dreaded Leyland cypress make a good background to work on. Small fir cones, especially sprays of larch cones, silvered poppy or teasel heads, and clusters of the tiny red hips from a rose such as 'Kiftsgate' will all look good. So will the silvered cases of beechnuts or ivy berry, together with bits of tinsel or baubles.

You can frost fir cones by dipping the top first into wallpaper paste, letting it dry until just tacky, then dipping it in a saucer of washing powder and scattering a bit of silver glitter on top of that. When dressing the wreaths, aim for a lush, fat effect. This is not the time for the minimal approach.

Silver spray paint is my greatest ally in the matter of Christmas decorations except when the nozzle jams, which happens with maddening frequency. It is worth collecting greenery the day before you want to spray it so that it can dry out. Paint will not stick to damp leaves. Ivy is at its best at Christmas. Not only are the leaves handsome but, on mature plants, you get clusters of berries which look terrific when sprayed.

I usually do a mountain of the stuff, then arrange silver-berried pieces of ivy all along the mantelshelf of the biggest fireplace, with candles at either end. In among the ivy goes a row of oranges, the biggest I can find, with a hole bored in the top of each one to take a short red candle. A strip of gold or silver ribbon round the waist of each orange enhances the effect. If the oranges wobble, jam some plasticine under them. Do not leave the candles burning if you are not in the room: ivy is very inflammable.

Silver ivy, or plain box or yew, looks handsome when made into hanging balls. Floral artistes will use balls of Oasis as the base. I generally use a roundish potato, although this is harder to pierce with stems of evergreen. It helps to make holes with a skewer first. Tie wire or string round the Oasis/potato like a parcel and fix a loop at the top for hanging before you begin. Then push greenery or silvered ivy into the ball all the way round, choosing pieces that are not straggly. Finish either with a ribbon at the top, like the holly wreath, or else jam in some baubles fixed on to florists' wire. Hanging on red ribbon, they look good beside a fireplace.

There is so much ivy in our garden that I never bother too much where I take it from. It is also fast-growing when it is established, and seems able to cover any gap between one Christmas and the next. You need to be much more circumspect with box and yew, however. Both are trees that demand respect and both are slow-growing. Cut carefully so that the tree does not look lopsided and do not always cut from the bottom of the tree unless you specifically want bare trunk. As with holly, make your cuts either flush with the trunk or where one branch meets another.

DECEMBER

Where there is no floor space for a Christmas tree you can get roughly the same effect by cutting branches of beech or hazel or any other gracefully twiggy tree and silvering them. Tie them together, not too tightly, and hang them upside down against the wall so that they lie flat and spread out in a fan-like arrangement. Then either train small coloured lights round the branches, or decorate with glass baubles and tinsel. The glaucous Atlas cedar (*Cedrus atlantica glauca*) also looks magnificent arranged like this. Its attractive bluish foliage will not need silvering.

Table decorations in our house are now strictly edible affairs. One Christmas I did try a sub-Constance Spry centrepiece making much use of thin Danish candles and artfully disposed pieces of silver ribbon. Most of it had to be summarily demolished to make way for twelve people and the turkey with all its outriders.

Since then we have relied on ad-hoc assemblies of exotic fruit, mixed with baubles, sitting on a bed of evergreen. It makes an alternative for anyone not able to face Christmas pudding. It also enhances the impression that during Christmas our place, with its swags of greenery, coils of vine and loops of ivy, resembles nothing so much as the set of some low-budget Tarzan movie. Next year we will get the chimpanzee.

An Expert History of Dr D. G. Hessayon

Green is how I felt, talking to Dr D.G. Hessayon, chairman of the chemical conglomerate pbi (Pan Britannica Industries) and author of the whole library of *Expert* books. If you haven't seen them – *The Rose Expert*, *The Lawn Expert*, *The Houseplant Expert* and others – you must just have returned from a life spent in Outer Mongolia.

The greenness had nothing to do with pbi's environmental Biofriendly range, everything to do with envy. It is galling to sit opposite a man who has sold 33 million copies of his books. Especially when he breezily tells you that writing is no more than a part-time occupation. I had not interviewed him for five and a half years. What, besides another eight million books sold, had happened in the meantime?

'Oh, I've mellowed,' he bellowed from the corner of the bar where we met. 'Mellowed considerably.' Some mellowing. The man is a walking explosion. The speech is as torrential as it ever was, the opinions as unshakeable. You get the history of Hessayon in ten and a half chapters before you have even taken off your coat. The modesty fairy forgot to call by at this particular cradle.

His office has prepared for the meeting by sending me a thick white bound document – *The Expert Author*, an introduction to Dr D.G. Hessayon. It

contains an awesomely impressive chapter on the sales figures of his books and a selection of off-the-shelf quotes. My favourite is the one that goes, 'I still find it hard to understand how *The Houseplant Expert* – which is 29 years old now – was the second-bestselling garden book in the three months before Christmas.' Not *that* hard, surely, Dr H.?

The document also contains excerpts from various book reviews. Hessayon shows the tiniest signs of disappointment about his reviews. He gets decent coverage in magazines such as *Garden Answers* and, he says, does well in the regional papers. He does not appear as often as he would like in the heavies. He puts it down to professional jealousy.

The books are brash and bossy. They are also authoritative, comprehensive and staggeringly good value for money. Hessayon is his own publisher and so avoids the inconvenience of an editor ruining his manuscript. He is also his own book designer. That is the bit he enjoys, dividing up sheets of paper with his coloured pencils, working out what should go where. He does most of the work in the basement of his house in Hertfordshire.

'I spend four months on the first stage,' he says. 'Then four months on the rest.' Pause. 'Which ain't bad, 'cos babies take nine.' Pause, because this quote does not appear in the handout and I am not writing fast enough. 'And similarly,' – another pause signals the punch line – 'the best fun is at the beginning.'

There is always a queue of designers on the phone, he says. They tell him about the four great design faults in the books and how, if only he would let them in on the act, they could improve sales for him. He loves stories like this: Hessayon against the universe, the plain man against the ponces. The joke is that he knows perfectly well there are umpteen design faults in the books. And split infinitives, hanging prepositions and sloppy punctuation to boot. But against all the disdainful carping he can set that one great, glittering, indisputable figure. Thirty-three million books, kiddo. Match that.

He was, he volunteers apropos of nothing in particular, born in the Year of the Dragon. I think, obliquely, it had to do with the takeover of his company by the Japanese giant Sumitoto a few years ago. My handbook of Chinese astrology sums up dragon people as magnanimous, full of vitality and strength, egocentric, eccentric, dogmatic, demanding, occasionally unreasonable, direct and never without a band of devoted admirers. That seems pretty well spot on to me. In his case, magnanimity and generosity weigh as heavily in the balance as any faults.

When he leaves his script, he is an engaging talker, though pungent rather than profound and fond of homespun philosophies. You wouldn't call him a conversationalist. He doesn't leave enough gaps for that.

DECEMBER

He has a magpie mind, strong on facts of the 'Fancy that' kind. One minute it is Robert Maxwell, the next the Bible. 'I'm an atheist, of course. You have to be to study the Bible properly. Otherwise it's like watching your own child in a school nativity play.'

Apropos of Maxwell, whom he knew, at least well enough to be invited to the Headington Hall birthday bashes, we talk about the psyche of the immigrant. 'If they won't let you play, you buy your own ball, play your own game,' he says. Was this what happened to him?

First he points out firmly that he was born in England, in Manchester. This was in 1928. His parents were Armenian/Cypriot. Then he thought there might be something in the theory. He is not the slightest bit interested in acquiring the trappings of English gentlemanliness. 'I'm amazed that people want to surround themselves with possessions. Why should I want a second home for instance? I have enough trouble with my first one. You're not halving your problems. You're doubling them.'

From there, it is an easy step to millionaires. I didn't ask him, but he must be one, what with those book figures and having sold the company and all. What was the common factor between all millionaires, he asked and plunged without pausing into the answer. It is not background, nor training, nor IQ. It is the ability to look on cash as a series of chips or counters, not as stuff that relates to the price of houses or a box of cornflakes.

What did cash mean to him, I wondered? 'Security,' he answered instantly. Not power. Power came from his position at pbi and he had enjoyed it. Now he intends to spend more time on books. He has kept pbi publications under his own control. The first *Expert* book was published in 1959 after another of those 'they told him it couldn't be done' sagas that Dr Hessayon so relishes.

The most recent book, *The Houseplant Expert*, is fatter than the norm. He is not entirely happy about that. Might his audience be frightened by bulk? His normal length is 128 pages. This is 256. The design remains unrepentantly the same. I think that is an important element in his success.

Given his sales figures, Hessayon's books must be bought by people who don't normally buy books. Perhaps they buy, not only because the books are good, but because they are not frightening. They are sold, too, in all sorts of outlets – ironmongers, garden centres – where you do not usually find books. That helps with the image.

'I'm going to give you a scoop,' he says, when he has finished telling me the sales figures for the old *Houseplant Expert* (a cool eight million). I wait, pen poised. 'Garden DIY,' he announces elliptically. I wait on. 'My next book. Garden DIY.' 'Ah!' I say,

DECEMBER

but I feel somehow I have let him down.

Teaching is his natural mode, though he didn't last long when he tried it for real at the University of Manchester. 'Unbelievably low boredom threshold,' he said in explanation. Manchester is where he got his PhD. He uses the doctor title rather formally on the fronts of his books, as though anxious for validation.

He is short on hobbies and does not list gardening among them in *Who's Who*. He points this out, not me. The Wild West is the only interest that has been more than passing. It's the heroic bit he is interested in: the fighting, the suffering, the ability of ordinary people to surmount impossible odds. He thinks one day he might write about Calamity Jane. If he's allowed back for another life, he wants to be a historian rather than a chemist.

That smacks of forward planning – anathema to him. 'I'm a windows man,' he says. 'A window suddenly opens in life, perhaps for 20 seconds. If you are sharp enough you'll see the opportunity there. If you have life all planned out, you'll miss the window. The saddest thing in the world is the 21-year-old, coming for an interview. You ask him if there is anything he'd like to know about the company. He asks about the pension scheme! The bloody *pension* scheme . . . !' The impossibility of such a thought brings him momentarily to a halt – but not for long.

After arguing the merits of organic versus inorganic chemicals and waltzing quickly round politics and conjuring (he has a good trick with sugar cubes) we finally face the $64,000 question. What is the secret of his success? 'I run away very quickly from anything I'm no good at,' he says. The corollary of that is that you need to be able to recognize what you *are* good at. He has. So Happy Christmas, Dr H. Here's to the next eight million!

～◈～

A Cautionary Tale of Cyclamen

Shops and garden centres are awash in December with poinsettias, cyclamen, azaleas, Christmas cacti and chrysanthemums, all crimped up to the nines and ready to be whisked off to their new homes for Christmas. It must be a grisly shock for them. Since birth they have been cosseted and fed, kept warm and amused. Then suddenly, wham, bang: they are loaded into a van and their cosy life in the polytunnel is brought to an abrupt end. There is no more capillary matting, no more temperature control, none of those little attentions to which a potted plant can so easily get accustomed.

Cyclamen, in particular, are not used to slumming it. Barely a quarter of them will adjust to the reduced circumstances in which Christmas usually finds them.

DECEMBER

In a test by *Gardening from Which?* only four out of fifteen cyclamen bought just before Christmas were still alive by the beginning of February, despite the expert attention of Consumers' Association members.

As a convicted cyclamen killer, I feel unqualified to give advice on keeping them alive, so I turned to the manager of the Van Hage Garden Centre, Great Anwell, near Ware, Hertfordshire – winner of the Garden Centre Association's award for the best houseplant department in the country.

First of all, do not buy plants that are standing outside in the cold. They do not like this any more than we do, although they are slower (and quieter) to show their displeasure. Look for plants that are compact, with healthy dark foliage, and choose those that have plenty of buds and not too many fully open flowers. That is as much as you can do if you are on the giving end of the present.

If you are on the receiving end, remember that cyclamen hate central heating and great fluctuations in temperature. A steady 50–55°F/10–13°C is what they need. Their compost should be just moist but not waterlogged. Never let the corm itself get wet: this is easily avoided if you soak the pot from below rather than sprinkling it from above. Good light is essential. Check rigorously for dying stems or leaves and pull them away from the corm as soon as you see them. Grey mould and other fungal bogeymen are always lurking ready to attack.

Chrysanthemums proved the easiest plant to please in the *Gardening from Which?* test. As a race, they are more amenable to doctoring than other plants. Left to themselves, chrysanthemums bloom only when the days are short. By juggling with available light and shade, commercial growers can now persuade flowers to grow at any time of the year. Pot chrysanthemums are also treated with a hormone dwarfing compound that keeps them at a neat and tidy 12in/30cm high.

If you bring them through Christmas successfully, you can plant them outside in spring where, untreated, they will grow up to their natural size. Look for sturdy plants, with no hint of yellow in the foliage. Buds should be showing colour but not fully open. On the other hand, if they are too tightly shut, they may never shift at all. Flowers will last longest in cool temperatures. Compost should not dry out.

Of the eleven million pounds usually spent on pot plants in the run up to Christmas, poinsettias take the lion's share. They are a particularly Christmassy colour and not widely available at other times of the year. The biggest problem with them, in my experience, is leaf drop. If this happens, you are left with a naked skeleton topped with red rags, an avant-garde scarecrow. Leaf drop in poinsettias is unfortunately

DECEMBER

like backache in humans. There are so many possible causes that it is difficult to make the correct diagnosis. It could be overwatering or underwatering. It could be a chilly draught. It could be poor light.

According to the Van Hage manager, the perfect conditions are these: temperature around 55–60°F/ 13–16°C, maximum light and not too much water. Red spider mite and mealy bug are likely to find your poinsettias before the Christmas holidays are over. Zap them with an insecticide before they become entrenched.

If you are buying, remember that the freshest plants will have unopened flowers. The flowers are the insignificant little yellowish bumps in the centre of the red things. The red things are not flowers but bracts, which are a specialized kind of leaf. They will not necessarily be red. Modern varieties have white or pink bracts. Prices vary more widely than with other pot plants and it will be worth shopping around for a decent specimen. Poinsettias are generally more expensive than chrysanthemums and cyclamen. You can get a good cyclamen in a 5in/12cm pot for almost half the price of a poinsettia.

Azaleas are also popular plants to give as presents, but those who succeed with them usually live in fairly arctic conditions indoors. By nature, azaleas are out-door woodland plants. They like cool, slightly damp growing conditions, not what you are most likely to find in a centrally heated flat. Azaleas are also acid lovers. Prolonged doses of alkaline tap water will not be to their liking. If you live in a hard-water area, use rainwater. If this is not feasible, use cold boiled water, give them frequent dunkings and misting over. Stand pots on a tray of damp pebbles to increase humidity.

A large azalea, although correspondingly more expensive, may in the end be a better buy than a small one. A large plant will have become well used to life in a pot. Small plants may have been potted up only a little while before being sold and, if so, will be less settled. Choose plants that have more buds than open flowers. If the foliage looks at all dry or is dropping from the branches, leave the plant just where it is on the shelf.

I once remarked to a garden-centre manager on the incontinent amount of leaf fall among his azaleas. He looked me straight in the eye and said, 'They always do that at this time of the year. You can't expect anything else.' Well they don't and you can.

If you are very talented you will be able to keep your azalea going for years. It will need to rest outside from April to September in a place that is cool and sheltered. When it goes outside, repot it in compost suitable for lime-haters and cut back any long, straggly shoots by half. Keep the pot well-watered and feed once a month with a fertilizer high in pot-

DECEMBER

ash. Bring it inside at the end of September before frosts threaten.

I am not a great fan of the Christmas cactus. I think I have had a surfeit of cuttings, ungainly bits of flattened leaf-like stem stuck in faded yogurt pots on the kitchen windowsill. It is quite unfair to write it off on such flimsy evidence but, even so, I hope nobody gives me one for Christmas, or at any other time. Certain sorts of shoes affect me in the same way – serviceable but dreary. By nature, Christmas cacti are epiphytes and grow clinging on to trees in the Brazilian jungle. They probably look splendid there and slightly sinister too, spilling out of the branches in bright green and pink. This is why they are sometimes recommended for hanging baskets. It seems a bad second best to me.

Amaryllis bulbs make excellent presents for children, because they grow very fast and have flowers that could have come straight from a Walt Disney cartoon. Kits, containing bulb, pot and compost, are relatively inexpensive. Instructions do not always suggest soaking the base of the bulb in lukewarm water for a few hours, but this does help to start the thing into growth. Keep the pot in a warm place and water sparingly until the flower stem starts to grow, then more generously. Flowers should appear about ten weeks after planting. And will nicely fill the gap left by the dead cyclamen.

THE POTAGER: PART FOUR
Staying Upright

The good intentions that you had if you started to think about a potager in the autumn now need to be translated into something slightly more urgent if the project is to get off the ground this season. Is the ground dug? Has the design been laid out? Has the design even been chosen? Are the seeds ordered? Get those things out of the way before you start on the December topic: planning the twiddly bits.

Everything that has so far been mentioned regarding the potager has happened at ground level. The plot will be far more effective if you also arrange some vertical events. Where these are to be fitted in will depend on the type of design you have adopted. If paths converge in the centre, some form of obelisk or arbour will emphasize this focus. Being in such an important position, a structure at the centre of your plot will draw the eye. This means that it has to be either good-looking or, if not, made in such a way that you can smother it with borrowed clothes.

It is worth thinking about the plants that you want to grow up, around or through a structure at the same time as you are thinking about the structure itself. The one has a bearing on the other. If you are dead set on runner beans as an extra crop in the potager, you will need a centrepiece made from separate poles or uprights. The beans, being twiners, need that sort of support.

Clematis hangs on by its leaf stalks. A smooth pole is not the easiest thing for it to get its mitt round. If you want to use clematis on its own to cover a centrepiece, choose a support with plenty of hand-holds, perhaps incorporating trellis or netting of some kind. You could make a centrepiece from fruit trees trained over a metal igloo-shaped frame.

If you decide on trained fruit as a centrepiece, think carefully about the variety. Pears are more malleable than apples. If apples, avoid boisterous varieties such as the Bramley cooker. It will soon outgrow a frame and never understand that, in the potager, small is beautiful. The disadvantage of fruit is that it is greedy. You will have to feed the soil well in order to be able to crop right up to the trunks of the trees. If the trees are trained over a small central paved area, they will not be in danger of shading crops.

The cheapest centrepiece will be a plant. A globe artichoke has the right dramatic credentials for the job, will look stunning from late May to October and will feed you. Unfortunately, like the dahlia, it is an all-or-nothing plant. When it is giving its all, it demands room – at least 4ft/1.2m in each direction. When it is nothing, it is a big nothing. And it is not fully hardy.

In a very small potager, a standard bay tree in a

decorative pot will be enough of a centrepiece. These are hideously expensive to buy (the plant, not the pot), but are formal, elegant and instant. The same can be said of a topiary centrepiece, but the bay has the edge in culinary terms.

Walk all the way round a prospective bay tree before you buy it to make sure that the head is well balanced on the stem. It will need regular feeding if it is in a pot. The prettiest are the ones trained as lollipops. To keep the shape, trim once or twice during the summer. You may also need to nip off suckers from the trunk.

There are, of course, other ways of using structures. By placing an arch or a pair of arches at the entrance and exit to the potager, you reinforce its difference from the rest of the garden. This is important in a small space. When you go under the arch, you enter a new country. The feeling is significant, even if the patch is fully open to view.

Arches of this sort also act as signals. If there are four ways in to the potager and you put arches over two of them, these will immediately appear more important than the others, even if all the paths are the same width. You can work this to your advantage. You may also be able to frame a view through the arches to another part of the garden. If the frame gives you nothing but the next door neighbour's washing line, plant a tree at the end of your view.

DECEMBER

If neither runner beans nor clematis appeal, think of a vine to cover the arbour or arch. The leaves are as important as any grapes you may get. The most dramatic member of the family, *Vitis coignetiae*, with hairy rounded leaves, will be too rampageous for an arch. Choose instead one of the *Vitis vinifera* tribe. 'Ciotat', the parsley vine, has deeply cut, fringed leaves – very pretty, but no good for stuffing. The fruits are small and black with a bluish bloom. 'Brant' has hand-shaped leaves which often colour well in autumn; the grapes are reddish purple. 'Purpurea' has fine dusty purple foliage, which makes an excellent background for any other flower you put with it.

Either cobaea or ipomoea (morning glory) would do. Both are annuals which you raise from seed and plant out at the end of May when they will not catch a chill. Cobaea climbs by means of pea-like tendrils. It is vigorous, but the flowers are often late getting into their stride. They are fleshy, purplish blue, like large Canterbury bells. The seed pods are extremely pretty, pale green and winged.

Sow the seed in late March or April, setting them one to a 3in/7.5cm pot. Harden off the plants before you set them to work. Morning glory, with blue convolvulus flowers, needs the same sort of treatment. Do not be tempted to set out the plants too early. Cold night temperatures cause the foliage to bleach and curl up. Sometimes the plants do not recover.

JOBS FOR THE MONTH

General

❀ Check that frost has not lifted the ground around newly planted shrubs and trees.

❀ Dig over heavy soil, leaving it in large clods to be broken down by frost.

❀ If necessary, shake snow from the branches of upright conifers to prevent them splaying out. A corset of large-mesh netting wrapped round the tree will prevent this happening in future.

Flowers

❀ Bring pots of bulbs into the warm when flower buds are showing through.

❀ Bring roses grown in containers into the greenhouse. Prune them hard while still under cover. This will encourage them to flower earlier than usual next season.

❀ Prune outdoor roses any time between now and early spring. The later time is safer in cold areas.

❀ Continue to plant roses, ensuring that the roots are well spread out in the planting hole. Firm the soil round the roots and mulch round the base of the plant.

❀ Continue to tidy beds and borders if the weather is kind.

❀ Pinch out the tips of sweet pea plants after the second or third pair of leaves appears.

❀ Indoor cyclamen are in full flood now. Unfortunately the conditions which they need to flourish are precisely those that are most difficult to provide in the average home. They like a cool temperature, somewhere around 55°F/13°C and bright light, but not direct sunlight. A north-facing windowsill usually suits them well. If the leaf stalks start stretching out in an ungainly way, the plant needs more light than it is getting. The compost should be moist but never wet. Keep water off the cyclamen tuber. Water by standing the pot in a bowl of slightly tepid water.

DECEMBER

❦ Amaryllis, because they grow so fast and have flowers as subtle as a heavyweight's punch, make excellent presents for children. Choose bulbs with thick firm roots. Before planting, soak the base of the bulb and roots in lukewarm water for a few hours. Plant in a pot that is only just big enough, leaving the top third of the bulb exposed. Keep the pot in the warm and water sparingly until the flower stem starts to grow. Amaryllis should flower ten weeks after planting.

❦ Hardware stores and garden centres often have half-price bulbs for sale at this time of the year. Tulips are a particularly good buy and will be least affected by late planting. Choose bulbs that are still plump and firm and avoid any that have begun to sprout. Look out for some of the early singles such as 'Apricot Beauty', darker inside than out, and 'Princess Margaret', a pink tulip fading to white at the base. Both are excellent in pots.

Vegetables

❦ Continue to spread manure on the vegetable garden, leaving one area unmanured. This is where you should grow root crops. If grown in freshly manured ground, carrots and parsnips fork into multiple roots.

❦ Harvest kohlrabi when the roots are about the size of a tennis ball.

Fruit

❦ Prune autumn-fruiting raspberries down to ground level.

❦ Prune vines when all leaves have fallen, reducing side shoots on mature plants to within one or two buds of the main stem.

ADDRESS BOOK

Plants and products mentioned in the articles in this book are available from the sources listed here. The following recommendations are by no means comprehensive, but single out some of the specialities mentioned earlier in this book. Note that not all of the firms listed offer mail order service, and some make a charge for their catalogues. All details were correct at the time of going to press.

Plant Suppliers and Seedsmen

Architectural Plants, Cooks Farm, Nuthurst, Horsham, West Sussex RH13 6LH (Tel 0403 891772) *excellent range of conservatory plants and exotica*

Aylett's, North Orbital Road, London Colney, St Albans, Herts (Tel 0727 22255) *dahlias*

B. & H. M. Baker, Bourne Brook Nurseries, Greenstead Green, Halstead, Essex CO9 1RJ (Tel 0787 472900) *fuchsias, but not mail order*

Peter Beales Roses, London Road, Attleborough, Norfolk NR17 1AY (Tel 0953 454707) *roses*

Tom Bebbington Dahlias, Lady Gate Nursery, 47 The Green, Diseworth, Derbyshire DE7 2QN (Tel 0332 811565) *dahlias*

Walter Blom & Son, Coombelands Nurseries, Leavesden, Watford, Herts ED2 7BH (Tel 0923 672071) *bulbs, especially tulips*

The Botanic Nursery, Rookery Nursery, Atworth, Melksham, Wilts SN12 8NU (Tel 0225 706597) *good range of lime-tolerant plants*

J. W. Boyce, Bush Pasture, Lower Carter Street, Fordham, Ely, Cambs CB7 5JU, *grass seed, excellent range of vegetables*

Cally Gardens, Gatehouse of Fleet, Castle Douglas, Scotland DG7 2DJ, *unusual perennials – eryngium, geranium, penstemon*

Carters Tested Seeds Ltd, Hele Road, Torquay, Devon TQ2 7QJ (Tel 0803 616156) *good general range*

Chiltern Seeds, Bortree Stile, Ulverston, Cumbria LA12 7PB, *wide general range, with interesting vegetables and herbs*

Donington Plants, Donington House, Main Road, Wrangle, Boston, Lincs PE22 9AT (Tel 0205 870015) *auriculas, penstemons, argyrantheums*

Fibrex Nurseries Ltd, Honeybourne Road, Pebworth, Stratford-upon-Avon, Warwicks CV37 8XT (Tel 0789 720788) *ferns and ivies*

Greater Dixter Nurseries, Northiam, East Sussex TN31 6PH, *clematis and unusual perennials*

Heritage Seeds, Henry Doubleday Research Association, National Centre for Organic Gardening, Ryton Gardens, Ryton-on-Dunsmore, Coventry CV8 3LG (Tel 0203 303517) *wide range of vegetable, herbs and flower seeds, plants and organic garden products*

W. E. Th. Ingwerson Ltd, Birch Farm Nursery, Gravetye, East Grinstead, West Sussex RH19 4LE (Tel 0342 810236) *a wide range of alpines*

P. de Jager & Sons, The Nurseries, Marden, Kent TN12 9BP (Tel 0622 831235) *bulbs*

Reginald Kaye Ltd, Waithman Nurseries, Silverdale, Carnforth, Lancs LA5 0TY (Tel 0524 701252) *ferns*

Keepers Nursery, 446 Wateringbury Road, East Malling, Maidstone, Kent ME19 6JJ (Tel 0622 813008) *fruit trees*

Kingsfield Conservation Nursery, Broadenham Lane, Winsham, Chard, Somerset TA20 4JF (Tel 0460 30697) *hedging plants and British native plants*

Langley Boxwood Nursery, Langley Court, Rake, Liss, Hants GU33 7JL (Tel 0730 894467) *many forms of box*

C. S. Lockyer, Lansbury, 70 Henfield Road, Coalpit Heath, Bristol, Avon BS217 2UZ (Tel 0454 772219) *fuchsias*

McBeans' Orchids, Cooksbridge, Lewes, Sussex BN8 4PR (Tel 0273 400228) *orchids*

Elizabeth MacGregor, Ellenbank, Tongland Road, Kircudbright DG6 4UU (Tel 0557 30620) *violas, violettas and violets*

Mallet Court Nursery, Curry Mallet, Taunton, Somerset TA3 6SY (Tel 0823 480748) *trees, including maples, oaks, hollies and other evergreens such as abies, myrtle, pine and sarcococca*

Markham Grange Nurseries, Long Lands Lane, Brodsworth, Doncaster, South Yorks DN5 7XB (Tel 0302 722390) *fuchsias*

S. E. Marshall & Co Ltd, Wisbech, Cambs PE13 2RF (Tel 0945 583407) *vegetable seed*

J. & D. Marston, Culag, Green Lane, Nafferton, Driffield, East Yorks YO25 0LF (Tel 0377 44487) *ferns*

New Trees Nursery, 2 Nunnery Road, Canterbury, Kent CT1 3LS (Tel 0227 761209) *fruit trees*

J. Parker Dutch Bulbs, 452 Chester Road, Old Trafford, Manchester M16 9HL (Tel 061 872 3517) *bulbs in wholesale quantities*

Pennells Nurseries, Newark Road, South Hykeham, Lincoln, Lincs LN6 9NT, *clematis*

Perrie Hale Forest Nursery, Northcote Hill, Honiton, Devon EX14 8TH (Tel 0404 43344) *hedging plants, native trees and shrubs*

Plants from the Past, The Old House, 1 North Street, Belhaven, Dunbar, East Lothian EN42 1NU (Tel 0368 63223) *unusual perennials, particularly old-fashioned kinds such as aquilegia, bellis etc*

W. Robinson & Sons Ltd, Sunnybank, Forton, near Preston, Lancs PR3 0BN (Tel 0524 791210) *mammoth vegetable seed, excellent range of tomatoes*

R. V. Roger Ltd, The Nurseries, Pickering, North Yorks YO18 7HG (Tel 0751 72226) *vegetable seed and wide general range*

Scotts Nurseries (Merriott) Ltd, Merriott, Somerset TA16 5PL (Tel 0460 72306) *good range of perennials, shrubs and trees, particularly fruit; hedging plants: beech, hornbeam, thorn etc*

Suffolk Herbs, Monks Farm, Pantlings Lane, Coggeshall Road, Kelvedon, Essex CO5 9PG (Tel 0376 572456) *herbs, unusual vegetables, conservation seeds, wild flowers*

Suttons Seeds Ltd, Hele Road, Torquay, Devon TQ2 7QJ (Tel 0803 612011) *wide general range of flowers and vegetables, plus grass seed*

Thompson & Morgan, London Road, Ipswich, Suffolk IP2 0BA (Tel 0473 688588) *good general range of seed*

Philip Tivey & Sons, 28 Wanlip Road, Syston, Leicester LE7 8PA (Tel 0533 692968) *dahlias*

Treasures of Tenbury Ltd, Burford House Gardens, Tenbury Wells, Worcs WR15 8HQ (Tel 0584 810777) *clematis and unusual perennials*

Unusual Plants, Beth Chatto Gardens, Elmstead Market, Colchester, Essex CO7 7DB (Tel 0206 822007) *good range of perennials, especially foliage plants*

Unwins Seeds Ltd, Histon, Cambridge CB4 4ZZ (Tel 0945 588522) *good general range*

Valley Clematis Nursery, Willingham Road, Hainton, Lincoln LN3 6LN (Tel 0507 81398) *clematis*

Van Hage Seed Specialists, Great Amwell, Ware, Herts SG12 9RP (Tel 0920 870811) *vegetables, good general range*

Garden Hardware

Agriframes Ltd, Charlswoods Road, East Grinstead, West Sussex RH19 2HG (Tel 0342 328644) *arches etc*

J. Alsford Ltd, Rye, East Sussex (Tel 0797 222501) *Osmo/gard timber treatment products*

Asian Affair, Castle Mills, King Street, Cleckheaton, West Yorks BD19 3JX, *glazed pots and planters*

Camland Products, Fordham House, Fordham, Cambs CB7 5LN, *bark in different grades*

Castacrete, Dean Street, East Farleigh, Maidstone, Kent ME15 0PS (Tel 0622 676098) *paving*

Conservation Building Products Ltd, Forge Works, Forge Lane, Cradley Heath, Warley, West Midlands B64 5AL (Tel 0384 69551) *old bricks, tiles etc*

ECC Building Products, Swindon, Wilts SN1 4JJ (Tel 0793 512288) *paving*

Frolics of Winchester, 82 Canon Street, Winchester, Hants SO23 9JQ (Tel 0962 856384) *ornamental 'Trellix' pyramids, unusual garden furniture*

Haddonstone, Forge House, East Haddon, Northants NN6 8DB (Tel 0604 770711) *reproduction stone urns, balustrades etc*

Hickson Landscape Structures, Wheldon Road, Castleford, West Yorks F10 2JT (Tel 0977 556565) *timber decking*

Jacksons Fencing, Stowting Common, near Ashford, Kent TN25 6BN; Chilcompton near Bath, Somerset BA3 4JE; Wrexham Road, Belgrave, Chester CH4 9ES, *large variety of fencing including hurdles, trelliswork and fixings*

Longlife Timber, 18 Fairfield Villas, Deighton Road, Wetherby LS22 4TN (Tel 0937 61620) *timber decking*

Metpost, Mardy Road, Cardiff CF3 8EQ, *spiked metal seatings for fenceposts etc*

Snapdragon, 268 Lee High Road, London SE13 5PL (Tel 081 852 0296); 167 Dawes Road, London SW6 (071 385 9866) *pots and planters*

Societies of Plant and Garden Interest

Auriculas etc: National Auricula and Primula Society, c/o Lawrence Wigley, 67 Warnham Court Road, Carshalton Beeches, Surrey SM5 3ND (Southern Section); David Hadfield, 146 Queens Road, Cheadle Hulme, Cheshire SK8 5NY (Northern Section); P. G. Ward, 6 Lawson Close, Saltford, Bristol BS18 3LB (Midland & West Section)

Clematis: International Clematis Society, c/o Mrs B. Risdon, The Tropical Bird Gardens, Rode, near Bath, Somerset

Dahlias: National Dahlia Society, c/o E. H. Collins, 19 Sunnybank, Marlow, Bucks SL7 3BL

Ferns: British Pteridological Society, c/o A. R. Busby, Croziers, 16 Kirby Corner Road, Canley, Coventry CV4 8GD

Fuchsias: British Fuchsia Society c/o R. Williams, 20 Brodawel, Llannon, Llanelli, Dyfed SA14 6BJ

Orchids: British Orchid Council, c/o A. J. Hainsworth, 20 Newbury Drive, Davy Hulme, Manchester M31 2FA; Scottish Orchid Society, c/o Mrs M. McFarlane, Grange View, Lamancha, West Linton EH46 7BD

Alpine Garden Society, c/o E. M. Upward, AGS Centre, Avon Bank, Pershore, Worcestershire WR10 3JP

Cottage Garden Society, c/o Mrs C. Tordoff, 5 Nixon Close, Thornhill, Dewsbury, West Yorks WF12 0JA; London Group: Mary Stickler, 7 Gwalior House, Avenue Road, Southgate, London N14 4DA (Tel 081 886 5959); Southeast Group: Mrs Hampshire, 10 Thorpe Close, Wokingham, Berks RG11 2PZ (Tel 0734 774 185)

National Gardens Scheme, Hatchlands Park, East Clandon, Guildford, Surrey GU4 7RT (Tel 0483 211535)

Recommended Reading

Peter Beales *Roses* (Harvill) 1992

Linda Brown *The Cook's Garden* (Century) 1990

Edward Hyams *English Cottage Gardens* (Penguin) 1987

Joy Larkcom *Oriental Vegetables* (John Murray) 1991

Christopher Lloyd *Clematis* (Viking) 1989

Christopher Lloyd and Graham Rice *Garden Flowers from Seed* (Viking) 1991

Prof. John Malins *The Essential Pruning Companion* (David & Charles) 1992

Brian Mathew *The Smaller Bulbs* (Batsford) 1987

Gerda Manthey *Fuchsias* (A & C Black) 1990

Dek Messecar *Pave It* (Collins) 1989

Alex Pankhurst *Who Does Your Garden Grow?* (Earl's Eye) 1992

The Plant Finder ed. Tony Lord (Headmain) published annually

Readers Digest *Encyclopaedia of Garden Plants* 1989

RHS *Gardeners' Encyclopaedia of Plants and Flowers* (Dorling Kindersley) 1989

RHS Wisley Handbook: *Vegetable Varieties for the Gardener* (Cassell/RHS) 1990

Graham Stuart Thomas *Perennial Garden Plants* (Dent) new ed. 1990

Peter Thompson *Creative Propagation* (Batsford) 1992

The Vegetable Finder (Henry Doubleday Research Association) 1992

The 'Yellow Book': *Gardens of England and Wales* (National Gardens Scheme) published annually

Index